U.S. ARMY PHOTO ALBUM

SHOOTING THE WAR IN COLOR
1941-1945 USA to ETO

Jonathan GAWNE

HISTOIRE & COLLECTIONS

Published by:
HISTOIRE & COLLECTIONS
5 avenue de la République
F-75541 Paris Cedex 11
France

Distributed in the U.S.A by:
Combined Books, Inc.
151 E. 10th Avenue
Conshohocken, PA 19248
Tel: 610-828-2595
Fax: 610-828-2603.

© Jonathan Gawne 1996

Designed and edited by Philippe Charbonnier.
Filmset by Arrigo
Printed and bound in France by Herissey
ISBN 2-908-182-40-8

This airborne photographer poses in the door of a grounded plane. The large rigger made bags just under the reserve chute probably were built to hold his spare photographic equipment. He has a light meter strapped to his right wrist for instant use. The 4x5 inch format Speed Graphic camera was the standard still photography camera used by the Signal Corps in WW2. If this man had tried to actually jump with the camera in hand as seen here, it likely would have pulled from his grip by the fast slipstream.

SHOOTING THE WAR IN COLOR, 1941-1945

Chapter One-Stateside training   5
Chapter Two-Italy and the Mediterranean   46
Chapter Three-The UK and Normandy   75
Chapter Four-Southern France   107
Chapter Five- Into Europe   113

INTRODUCTION

While researching black and white photographs in the National Archives I came across an index to a collection of color WW2 US Army Signal Corps photos. Asking the staff about them I was told they "weren't very interesting as none of them were combat shots". Taking a chance I looked through the dull, muted tones of the color prints in the collection. Someone, back in the days when the Pentagon had housed the collection, had left a few of the original transparencies in with the prints. I was astounded to look at clear, crisp color that might well have been taken the day before. I knew I had to get them published. Little did I know it would take many years to finally get them into print.

Unfortunately, the last 50 years have taken their toll on this collection. Some of the transparencies have been lost, others have started to fade or deteriorate. This collection is one of the greatest photographic treasures of WW2, yet it remains little known, poorly indexed, and in dire need of attention. Years of indifferent government care at the Pentagon have caused untold damage. Fortunately it is now in the hands of the Still Picture Branch of the National Archives. Most of the transparencies (but not all) are now in cold storage. Hopefully someone will find funding in the near future to properly sort, index, and make new study prints of this collection.

There are a great number of people which I have to thank for their help. Most importantly I have to thank Frank Errigo, Morris Berman, and Mrs. Norma Miller for sharing their stories of how the Army was shot in color. Countless veterans have put up with my constant questions about minute details of their military service. Betty Hill and her entire staff at the National Archives put up with endless demands for help and pulls from the cold room. Historians like Steve West and George Ghastly made me realize that some people care about quality work. My family endured my erratic behavior as well as stacks of slides, notes and photocopies scattered around the house. Philippe Charbonnier, more than anyone else, made it all happen.

Color Photography in the U.S. Army

The Eastman Kodak Company released their second version of Kodachrome color transparency (slide) film to the public on April 5th, 1935. They had previously marketed a cruder form of color film called Kodachrome in 1914, but the poor color reproduction resulted in low sales. Color photographs even pre-date the 1914 release, as many different types of experimental color films were sold after the first successful test of a color film in 1861. A handful of color 'Autochromes' from WW1 exist, but sadly the US Army never made use of this process.

The German film company Agfa had released their own version of color film in the 30's. It was not as sharp as Kodachrome, but served to record the German military in victorious color. Kodachrome and Agfachrome used different formulas, but Kodak's was better. The public got a taste of what was to come when National Geographic printed their first color photograph in April 1938. In 1942 Kodak released a color print film: Kodacolor. The quality was not very good, and Kodachrome remained the color film of choice. There is no evidence that the military ever used Kodacolor for anything more than a few film tests.

The U.S. Army actually experimented with Agfa stocks, but found the film did not hold up to rough handling the way Kodachrome did. Agfachrome was more susceptible to damage from humidity and fungus. The Kodachrome film speed was slow: only 10 ISO (ASA), but it was the first commercially viable film that allowed for sharp and realistic color. As the public started to take notice of this new and exciting product, war broke out. Production of Kodachrome for civilian photography stopped for the duration.

Almost the entire wartime production of Kodak film went to the government. Photos were needed for aerial shots, training manuals, ID cards, and most of all publicity. While there were some limited uses for color film in training and evaluating camouflage, the Army started taking color photos specifically to supply the demands of civilian magazines that found that a color photo on the cover meant better sales. Color photography was originally under control of the War Department Bureau of Public Relations rather than the Photographic Branch of the Signal Corps.

The first Army color photographers selected were former instructors for the Signal Corps photography school. Once assigned to shoot color, they then took their orders from Army Public Relations rather than the Signal Corps. This shows that the Army saw color photographs as a P.R. tool rather than any kind of historical document. The photographers set up their shots so the pictures could stand alone as a poster image. This meant that they would be perfectly suited for magazine covers.

The majority of Army photography was done in a 4x5 inch format (mostly with Speed Graphic cameras). Some of the Army transparencies, mostly for portraits, were shot on large 8 x 10 inch sheets of film. It was not until late in the war that the smaller 35mm cameras caught on. A few rolls of 35mm film found their way into the Signal Corps Collection: namely from the beaches at Salerno, the loading of troops for Normandy, and the ruins of Saint-Lô. Due to the slow film speed, types of camera used, and difficulty in processing the film, the photographers often had to stage their shots to make every photo count. One photographer said that the rule of thumb was that he shot 35mm or 2 1/4 x 2 1/4 in the frontlines, 4x5 behind the lines, and 8x10 for portraits of officers and celebrities.

Black and white film was developed in the field or in local labs by photo units. The best negatives were captioned on site and shipped back to the States for addition to the official Signal Corps collection. Color

Ardean Miller (left) and Frank Errigo (right) are shown while photographing in Wyoming. For them it was a joke shot, because the camera is a newsreel motion micture camera, not equipment they generally used. These men were the first official color photographers authorized by the U.S. Army.
(Courtesy Frank Errigo)

film had to be processed by the Kodak plant, so exposed color film was shipped in sealed containers back to the Pentagon. Then it went straight to Rochester, New York where Kodak technicians processed it and sent it back to the Pentagon to pass the censors. Once checked for possible security breaches, such as showing a new type of weapon, it would be finally passed on to the Army Pictorial Library in the Pentagon. In most cases the color photographer never saw the results until much later. This resulted in a number of captioning problems.

The photographers

Frank Errigo entered the Army as an advanced amateur in photography. He was sent to still photography classes, and then trained in motion picture skills in Hollywood under the guidance of Colonel Darryl Zanuck. He ended up at the Army Pictorial Service based at the Army War College at Ft. McNair, Washington DC.

His partner, Ardean Miller III, came from a very solid background in color photography. He had worked for Eastman Kodak before the war as one of their principal color photographers. He took the color photographs of the 1939 World's Fair in New York, and had won a Leica Medal for his work. He tried to enlist in the Army, but was turned down for bad eyesight. A while later he was drafted and placed in the Signal Corps. After he entered the Army he was spotted in a Morse code class by General Ted Curtis (a former Kodak administrator given a direct commission into

the Signal Corps). The General realized he had one of the most experienced color photographers in the world under his command. Miller was pulled out of the Morse code class (leaving classmate William Holden, the actor) and teamed up with Errigo.

In 1943 Sergeants Errigo and Miller travelled around the various bases in the USA photographing the different branches of service. Their travels give some clue as to the locations of their photographs. Engineer shots were taken at Ft. Belvoir, Quartermaster shots at Ft. Francis Warren, Infantry at Ft. Benning, and the Coast Artillery and 7th Armored Division were taken in California. The Desert Training Center in Indio, California was the location for most of the desert shots. Amphibious training was taken at Camp Bradford.

Between trips the two photographers took on other assignments, including portraits of important government and military officials. One of their favorite stories was about photographing General 'Vinegar Joe' Stillwell. The General obviously thought this photo taking business was a waste of his time. The photographers dashed about replacing flash bulbs, checking light meters, changing film plates, and snapping photos. They suggested that he pick a pen and pretend to write something. When the film was developed they could read that the General had written "*this is a hell of an operation*" on the piece of paper.

In the Winter of 1943 the Army Signal Corps decided it needed color photos from overseas. The Pictorial Branch decided to send two color photographic teams to Europe. After a few lectures in color photography, a Signal Corps class was sent to an airfield and told to take their best photographs. As a result the two most promising students, Albert Norris 'Steve' Stevens and Morris Berman, were selected to join Errigo and Miller overseas. They were supposed to be on a 90 day special mission, but it would last until the war ended.

'Steve' Stevens apparently had no previous photography experience before he joined the Army, but Morris Berman had been a news photographer for the Pittsburgh Sun Telegraph. His draft board had given him a deferment so he could apply for a position as a civilian war photographer for a news service. The numerous background checks that had to be made by

Somewhere in Europe, this photo was taken of Ardean Miller (left), 'Steve' Stevens on the command car, and correspondent 'Red' Gaston at right. Miller and Stevens travelled from England through France and into Germany taking color photographs. Both men were Sergeants, but the lack of rank insignia allowed them the advantage of no one really knowing what rank they were, or if they were civilian photographers. The front of their command car is decorated with a bottle of Champagne, a shattered German helmet, and a minefield warning sign.
(Courtesy Mrs. Ardean Miller)

Marlene Dietrich became fascinated by a large 8x10 inch camera used by the photographers to take pictures of her. After her performance at a U.S.O. show in Italy she told them that she wanted to take a picture of the photographers for a change. This photograph shows Dietrich using the 8x10 camera to photograph Frank Errigo at far right, and Morris Berman in the center. The soldier on the left was Dietrich's USO liaison to the Army. Errigo and Berman were the photographic team responsible for most of the color photography taken in the Mediterranean.
(Courtesy Morris Berman)

the F.B.I. were dragging on, and Berman saw the Allies quickly wrapping up the fighting in North Africa. Worried that the war might end before he got overseas, he went back to his draft board and had them induct him immediately.

While Berman was entering military life, Dick Sarno was a Signal Corps officer at the 3225th Signal Photo Center desperate for trained photographers. The 3225th was based at the former Paramount film studio in Astoria, New York. Sarno called every major newspaper he could, asking if they knew of any press photographers that had been drafted. He found out about Berman and officially requested him through channels to be assigned to the 3225th.

Once in North Africa, Errigo and Berman were held up by red tape. Although they were on detached service from the Army Photographic Service, they were assigned to the 163rd Signal Photographic Company (SPC) for administrative purposes. The 163rd was so short of equipment that its commander, Captain Ned Moorehouse, kept Errigo and Berman in North Africa so he could appropriate their equipment. When the Senior Signal Corps Photographic Officer in the Mediterranean, Colonel Melvin Gillette, found out about this he soon had Errigo and Berman on their way to photograph the war in Italy. The 163rd would supply them with a jeep and driver, as well as provide a base of operations for food, mail, and film. Often a motion picture cameraman from the 163rd would accompany them taking 35mm black and white movie footage.

For the most part the two teams appear to have been left on their own to capture whatever photographs they felt would work best in color. From time to time a specific assignment would be given to them, such as documenting the evacuation of wounded from Anzio. This would have been an important morale boosting tool to show how quickly and well American wounded were taken care of. After the photographs had been taken, one of the photographers

would type up captions for their work, and the exposed film would be shipped by air to the States. There it would be processed by Kodak and sent to the Army Pictorial Library in the Pentagon. Approximately a week after taking the photos, the men would receive a report on how well they had done. Generally these reports only contained details about how well the film had been exposed.

There was an interesting side note to the film library at the Pentagon. One of the receptionists was Ardean Miller's wife. Mrs. Miller had grown up near the Kodak plant in Rochester New York, and had actually been the very first woman to be photographed on Kodachrome film when she was about 13 years old. She continued to work as a model for Kodak and had married Ardean before the war, then followed him to Washington when he worked at the Army War College.

Miller and Stevens had been sent to England to await the Normandy Invasion. It appears they were attached to the 165th SPC for their administrative support. Miller was the photographer that shot the Paris photos and the link up between Soviet and American troops. Stevens took shrapnel in his leg while trying to cover one battle, but the wound was mild enough that he did not stay out of action. At some point the two men separated, with Stevens staying in Germany, while Miller worked out of Paris. His wife later remarked that photographing Buchenwald was something that would haunt Ardean for the rest of his life. Perhaps this is the reason he chose to leave Germany and return to Paris.

At the end of the war Miller heard that the Germans were about to surrender in Rheims. In the middle of the night he drove to the city, but was told that nothing would happen until much later. Determined to not miss the shot, he slept under the table where the surrender would be signed. Later that day he stood behind Field Marshal Jodl for the surrender document signing. Weeks later Mrs. Miller was thrilled when she saw the newsreels of the surrender. Ardean Miller is shown with his Speed Graphic standing right behind Jodl.

Down in the Mediterranean Errigo and Berman worked their way up to the liberation of Rome where they were the first photographers to have a private audience with the Pope. After Rome was liberated, Berman and Errigo took photos of George Marshall's visit to Italy, Clark's headquarters, and the Japanese-American Nisei. Errigo had been thrown 40 feet by an artillery blast at Anzio. In the fall of 1944, because of complications from the blast effect, Errigo was sent back to the United States to work on developing color coverage in the Pacific. No special Army color

photography teams would go to the Pacific, and Errigo spent the rest of the war shooting subjects in the Washington DC area.

At one point Berman was photographing an engineer unit experimenting with a method of breaching a minefield by firing an explosive cord into the mine field. When detonated the cord was to have cleared a safe path through the minefield. Unfortunately, there were more mines than expected and Berman suffered minor wounds to his hands from the explosion. With no other color photographers available, he continued to cover the Italian Front until the end of the war.

With his news reporter's skill, he was there to record the aftermath of Mussolini's hanging and mutilation. He recalled "as soon as the bodies were cut down the undertaker rushed out and put a toe tag on them- as if there was any question as to who they were." With Berman in Northern Italy, and Errigo back in the States there was no Army color photographer to cover the landings in Southern France. Fortunately, an unknown Navy photographer took a few shots along the landing area.

After the war all four men would stay in photography. Frank Errigo went to work for the *Philadelphia Enquirer*, and later for the Armstrong floor and ceiling company. Morris Berman was one of the founding members of the International Freelance photographers association, and specialized in sports photographs. Ardean Miller and 'Steve' Stevens continued to work together as a freelance photography team for many years until, sadly, Stevens was killed in a commercial plane crash. His files, which possibly contain some unique color material from the ETO, remain missing and presumed lost.

Captions for the photographs are a problem. In most cases the official captions are some insipid mention of 'Tanks training for combat' or 'Brave GI's moving forward'. In some cases the captions are just plain wrong. It appears that the original captions made by the photographers were sometimes drastically changed by the censors. Most unit names are not mentioned, and sometimes the only date provided is the date of declassification and release to the public - not of the actual photography. This means that photos of pre-D-Day England can be dated 1946. It is a long process to figure out the when, where, and who of the photograph. Since most of the dates stamped on the captions do not seem to have any bearing to the actual day of shooting, they have not been included in this book unless there is other corroborating evidence in the photo.

There are still a great many color photographs in the collection that are not included here. Many are boring - showing a famous building, or a forgotten Colonel in his nameless office. A number have deteriorated to a point where they are hazy images with no color left.

Anyone interested in the activities of the military photographers (not to be confused with civilian press photographers) should read Peter Maslowski's excellent book 'Armed With Cameras' (ISBN 0-0292-0265-5). He covers photographers in uniform from all of the different branches of service.

After years of staring at black and white photographs trying to figure out what shade of olive drab a jacket is, or what color band was painted on MP helmets, these color photographs are a joy to behold. Unless you have access to original artifacts, it can be difficult trying to figure out what color OD shade #7 really is. Every effort has been taken to try and preserve the colors of the original transparencies in this book. In some cases the originals have started to fade, but the photos have been included anyway for the information they still contain. With the increasing interest in WW2, one can only hope that the remaining color images will be taken care of and preserved.

Jonathan Gawne

Right.
The American sergeant: the backbone of the Army. This sergeant wears the basic uniform of WW2. The wool shirt and trousers were standard in almost every theater of the war. He carries the M1 Garand rifle, the first semi-automatic rifle adopted by any army as the standard firearm. 'Buck' sergeants started out the war as squad leaders, but in December 1943 the rank structure was altered so staff sergeants commanded squads, moving the sergeant to the position of assistant squad leader.

Below.
General of the Army George C. Marshall gets little credit for the important role he played in WW2. As the Chief of Staff of the Army he was responsible for how the war was fought, and eventually the man responsible for victory. He is often neglected by many who prefer to study battlefield generals who won victories using the doctrine and weapons developed through his foresight. Marshall was commissioned as a lieutenant in 1902, and served in many areas-from the Philippines to China. In WW1 he went to France with the 1st infantry Division, and then became chief of operations for the First Army. As Commandant of the Infantry School at Ft. Benning in the early 1930's, he had a great impact on the development of the U.S. Army.

STATESIDE TRAINING

Above.

Standing in line, whether for chow or any other reason, has always been a major part of any Army. Most of the men pictured here wear the olive drab herring bone twill (HBT) fatigue uniform with the wide brimmed hat. This uniform was developed to be worn for dirty jobs (known as 'fatigue duty' in the Army), and sized large to go over the wool uniform. The mess truck was set up so that the cooks could work in the back while the truck was on the road.

Right.

In the first years of the war, much of the training was based on experiences of WW1. Here two men attempt to cut their way through a belt of barbed wire. Of particular interest is the flat 1917A1 helmet, only slightly better than the WW1 version, and the extreme fading seen in their web equipment. In all probability it has been in use since the end of WW1, much like the bolt action rifles they are using. They wear the special barbed wire gauntlets to protect their hands.

Above right.
Wearing the full M-1928 infantry haversack, this soldier wears the old style blue denim fatigues. The Army started to phase out these blue fatigues in 1938, but it was not until 1941 that the changeover to OD HBT was accomplished. The haversack was only slightly modified from the WW1 pack, and the design was universally hated by GI's because of the difficulty they had in packing it. At the bottom the pack carrier is attached, which was used to extend the amount of equipment carried. He is using an EE-8 field telephone and wears a right side holster for the 1917 .45 caliber pistol.

Right.
Wearing the blue denim fatigue trousers and standard white sleeveless undershirt, this soldier attempts to cook a meal on a makeshift stove. The mess kit and canteen cup remained little changed from WW1, but for the most part food improved as the war went along. In the 30's soldiers in the field were basically limited to beans, hardtack and bacon as field rations. This changed to a wider variety of canned food as WW2 progressed.

Above.
Almost unchanged from 1918, these artillerymen with a 75mm pack howitzer wear wool breeches. Their riding boots and spurs indicate that this is still a horse drawn unit. All that differs from their father's uniform is the newer service gas mask worn on the left hip. Even the web equipment is of WW1 vintage, as the first aid pouch seen on the central figure is clearly the double snap WW1 variety. Within a year of this photo being taken this unit probably traded in their horses for trucks.

Left.
These signalmen wear the standard field uniform of wool shirts and trousers with canvas leggings. The heavy, but portable, BD-71 switchboard was able to handle six field telephone lines. This photo was taken pre- December 1942, as the men wear black ties. After that date the Army changed over to a tan necktie for all troops. The corporal at right is using a Morse code telegraph set TG-5 which sits on a large DR-4 wire reel.

Below.
Under the broken shadows of a camouflage net, the crew of a 240mm gun ram a yellow painted shell into the breech. Due to the large size of the shell the powder bags would be handled separately and placed in the gun behind this projectile. Before the war all explosives were painted yellow as a safety measure. This was changed to olive drab for camouflage reasons during the war.

The yellow painted ammunition is clearly visible for what appears to be a 90mm anti-aircraft gun. This crew wears the HBT fatigue uniform in various stages of fading. Many coastal artillery units were converted into anti-aircraft units such as this. When the Luftwaffe was destroyed, the gun crews were rapidly re-trained as infantry replacements. At the lower left one man wears the patch of the General Headquarters Reserve.

Below.
Tractor drawn 155mm guns on the move during the 2nd Tennessee maneuvers of 1942. The second tractor in line - an International Harvester TD 18 - hauls a trailer filled with ammunition and other equipment. Heavy tractors had been developed to haul artillery pieces through the churned up mud of WW1. All but the heaviest of guns would be hauled by the more powerful modern trucks in WW2.

Right.
The main infantry anti-tank weapon in 1942 was the 37mm gun. It proved to be basically useless and the popular opinion was that it wouldn't even scratch the paint off a German tank. It was replaced with the larger 57mm anti-tank gun in mid 1943, just in time for the invasion of Italy.

Above.
Early experimental hand painted camouflage uniforms are seen here at one of the desert training areas in the southwest United States. Before the Army settled on a standard camouflage uniform, there were a number of trials to determine what the best pattern and coloration should be. The 'hidden' men in the foreground are from one of those tests, and wear painted HBT uniforms. With the decision to invade North Africa, many units were sent to one of these Southwest camps for training in desert warfare.

Left.
Physical toughening continued to be an important element of military training, and these men are probably on a forced march across a rough landscape, which will also teach them the rudiments of climbing. They wear the cooler HBT cotton fatigues, and are probably vehicle crews as they wear the M36 musette bag instead of the infantry haversack.

Left.
The halftrack at another of the desert training camps belongs to the 4th Armored Corps (note the Roman numeral on the bumper). Obviously a staged shot for the camera, one wonders if the camouflage scattered around the vehicle was not removed on purpose to provide a better view of it for the photo. The burlap strips in the cammo net are of a much lighter shade than normally found on vehicle nets used in the ETO.

Above.
The one-piece camouflage jungle suit was developed for fighting in the Pacific, but did see limited use in the ETO. The color scheme of this uniform was reversible with one side being brown, and the other more greenish. The official name of the cammo pattern was 'frog-skin'.

Another fanciful photograph is this 1917A1 machine gun position hidden under a fake rock. The crew wears paint spattered fatigues as camouflage, while the rock appears to have been constructed of a paper-mache over a screen and wooden frame. One problem with hiding this gun was that as it fired a thin stream of steam escaped from the hose fitting, and the crew ended up with a finger of steam pointing right down on their position. The ammo boxes are the early wooded variety which was rapidly replaced with a more rugged steel version.

Above.
An 81mm mortar crew from the 158th Infantry regiment in Puerto Rico. This photo shows a mixture of old blue and new OD fatigues. The high explosive shells on the ground are painted in the early war yellow color. The gunner on the left of the mortar aims it, while the assistant gunner on the right side drops the shell at the gunner's command. Behind the mortar an ammo bearer keeps feeding shells to the senior ammo bearer, whose job is to prep the shells for firing and then hand them to the assistant gunner. There were six 81mm mortars in each infantry heavy weapons company.

Previous page, top.
Appearing from a hidden 'spider hole' these two men wear the standard Army pattern camouflage 1-piece uniform with helmet cover. One carries the 1903 Springfield rifle, which was used extensively in the early stages of the war, but more likely pictured here for its ability as a highly accurate sniper's weapon. Photographs such as this were not only more colorful than the standard drab uniform, but caught the imagination of the public that felt their boys could fight without being seen. In practice the cammo uniform was withdrawn from use in the ETO after briefly being used by elements of the 2nd Armored division: too many troops had been conditioned to fire on anyone in cammo as '*only Germans wore camouflage uniforms*'.

Right.
This soldier with 1928 Thompson sub-machine gun peeps out from underneath a camouflage net. This weapon was time consuming to manufacture so the Army developed a simplified version, the M1A1, later on in the war. His goggles give him away as a vehicle crewman, probably from the halftrack seen on a previous page. The colors of the cammo nets are particularly interesting, with the darker two colors in the center the most common and the lighter issued for desert regions.

CHEMICAL WARFARE

Below.
Chemical warfare was a real threat for most of the war and American troops were given extensive training in the use of gas masks. Not only are these soldiers supposedly safe from gas, but so is their canine friend. Every regiment had a gas officer whose job it was to make sure the men were ready to defend against chemical attacks-and this frequently meant tossing tear gas grenades at the most unexpected times. The reel of field telephone wire has been tied to the dog's harness so he can pull out the wire to an advanced post without exposing a soldier to enemy fire. The dog shown here is actually the original TV star 'Rin Tin Tin'. The owner lent him to the photographers for these shots.

Left.
These Chemical Warfare Service soldiers wear the impermeable protective suit while filling M47 100 pound chemical aircraft bombs. Impermeable suits, rather than an impregnated wool uniform, were needed when working with mustard gas. The M47 bomb was specifically designed to deliver mustard gas (which is a liquid not a gas) to the battlefield. The yellow color indicates it is 'live ' and not a dummy bomb.

Right and below.
Every soldier carried an individual protective cover as defense against contact chemical weapons such as mustard gas. The disposable plastic bag folded into the size of a paperback book, and was transparent at the top so the soldier could see to protect himself even when under chemical attack. Every man was supposed to carry two of these. They were very useful as temporary raincoats, or in making rainproof shelters.

Above.
This early GMC AF361 Signal Corps radio truck pulls the generator needed to power it in the trailer. As the war progressed, radio equipment shrunk drastically in size and weight while power and range increased. This kind of mobile radio system would only be found at higher headquarters far back from the fighting. The registration numbers are painted in light blue, the regulation color for the early stages of the war.

Above.
This switchboard operator is working at the BD-71 six drop (or six circuit) switchboard. It comes with folding legs, and although a bit heavy, was considered very portable. The reel of wire on top of the switchboard is connected to a TS–10 sound powered field phone. Instead of cranking a bell to signal the other end, the user of this phone would have to whistle loudly into it to announce a call was being made. This phone was very lightweight, and the most common one used by front line troops.

Right.
This radio operator from the 5th Armored Division wears his unit patch over his heart, where General Patton felt it should be. Unlike the rest of the Army, some armored units had a habit of wearing their patch on the left chest of their fatigue jacket or overalls. Normally insignia is not worn on the fatigues at all. The uniform is a first pattern HBT coverall (from the pocket flap), and the helmet liner is the early thick, cloth covered fiber liner. On the handset can be seen the orange colored Signal Corps acceptance stamp. Slung on his left hip is the standard service gas mask.

The US Army made extensive use of training films to help turn civilians into soldiers. Here we see a film on the importance of communications being shot on a sound stage *(top)*. The information on the slate shows that the photo was taken in October 1942. In another location a jungle has been built indoors to show what warfare is like in that environment. Obviously taken before the development of the issue camouflage uniform, hand painted camouflage on HBT uniforms are used- a sign that this kind of uniform would have been authorized to make on a unit level. Although a similar helmet cover has been made, neither the leggings or service gas mask bag has been painted.

HOLLYWOOD GOES TO WAR

Left.
The explosion of a white phosphorous grenade is dramatically shown here. This grenade was used for incendiary purposes, as well as creating a temporary smoke screen. The small particles of phosphorous kept burning, even when doused with water, making this a fearsome weapon to use against infantry. The man on the left shows how an HBT uniform can fade after repeated washings. Both men carry their raincoats strapped under the top flap of the haversack, which was common practice.

Above.
Even in the modernized U.S. Army traditional bayonet training was still given. These men, training with 1903 Springfield rifles, show an unusual mixture of blue denim and OD HBT fatigue uniforms. Most wear the wide brimmed HBT hat, but the two men in the foreground wear what resembles the Air Force summer flying cap. All have left the scabbards on their bayonets as a safety measure. In the background can be seen a few bayonet training devices that were used to teach recruits how to parry an enemy bayonet.

Left.
This WW1 era M1917 tank was good only to be used for anti-tank practice. Here a molotov cocktail is thrown at a stationary target to built confidence in fighting Panzers. The cocktail was a glass bottle filled with gasoline, and a rag tied around the neck. The rag was lit, the bottle thrown, and the burning gasoline would run down into the engine compartment.

As combat veterans returned to help train recruits, realism became more important. In this early version of a combat village men learn how to clear buildings. They wear the typical training uniform of HBTs, M1928 haversack, ammo belt, canteen and first aid pouch. Why two of them carry .45s in addition to their M1 Garands is a mystery, but they may be instructors helping stage the photograph

Below.
Crawling under barbed wire has become a traditional part of all military training. Here a .30 caliber light machine gunner works his M1919A4 under a belt of wire. By his left elbow can be seen the pintle that fits into the socket on the tripod. Later in the war the Army would re-design this gun to be fired from a permanently attached bipod, instead of needing a second man to carry the tripod.

Right.
This photograph shows the short range a flamethrower has. The operator has to get very close to his target, all the time carrying a large amount of highly flammable liquid on his back. All it takes is one bullet into the tanks and it all goes up in flames.

Previous page, top.
The bangalore torpedo was a 5 foot long metal pipe 2 $\frac{1}{8}$ inches in diameter and filled with explosives. When detonated under barbed wire, it would cut a path through the wire. Each section of torpedo could be joined to another to clear a deep belt of wire. Clearly seen here is the special pointed nose cap put on the tip of the torpedo to make sure the normally flat end does not hang up on any obstruction. Once the torpedo was in place the troops would pull the detonator starting a slow fuse and quickly run for cover.

Below.
The M1 flamethrower is seen in use by men wearing camouflage uniforms. This is the type of flamethrower carried on D-Day; although there has been no confirmed use of the weapon on either U.S. invasion beach. The helmet covers appear to be of an unusual locally painted variety. The man on the bottom carries a dummy pole charge ready to thrust it into the pill box opening once the flame has driven the occupants to cover.

Below.
Perhaps the most terrifying weapon of all was the flamethrower. It was terrifying not only to the enemy, but to the men that operated them. This M2 model was adopted in March 1944. It was superior to the early M1, but still needed a trained man to safely handle it. The backwards thrust of the weapon could easily push a man over if he did not fully lean forward before firing. He is covered by two Browning automatic rifles, whose job would be to drive the pill box occupants away from the opening long enough for the flamethrower to get in range.

Left.
The engineers had a wide variety of tasks to perform. Although some units would specialize in a specific job, everyone had to know the basics of any task they might be called upon to perform. Here an engineer unit constructs a bridge out of wood and metal beams. The dark russet brown color of the well polished service shoe is clearly visible. Later on this boot would be changed to a rough out finish that stood up better to combat wear, but did not hold a polish as well.

Below.
'*Fire in the hole!*' is the traditional cry when setting off explosives. Here an engineer uses the ten cap blasting machine, fired with a sharp twisting motion, to set off a charge. The wire on his reel is standard for this kind of electrical detonation, and colored so it would not be mistaken as anything else but 'firing wire'. The color prevented anyone from accidentally attaching a field telephone to firing wires. The wire reel is also a different model from a telephone wire reel and holds 500 feet of firing wire. Slung from his body is not only a Garand rifle and service gas mask bag, but also a galvanometer- basically an ohm meter used to test that an electrical circuit is still intact before firing. At his left foot is a reel of primacord and around his right shoulder is a coil of smooth surfaced orange safety fuse.

Below.
Blue was the standard color for unloaded practice ammunition. This M1 anti-tank mine has a yellow stripe and spider for added visibility. The engineer in his mackinaw (issued to engineers in place of the standard field jacket) has dug out a hole to place the mine and put the dirt in a sandbag. He is now putting a booby trap below the mine, so that anyone trying to lift the mine will be in for a nasty surprise. When finished he will cover the mine up and carry the excess soil to another location for disposal.

Above.
The 105mm M3 howitzer was issued to the cannon company of all infantry regiments. Six of these guns were supposed to give the regiment some heavy hitting firepower right up on the front line, but in practice units preferred to use them as additional artillery and bring up more mobile tanks to provide close in fire support. The M3 was essentially a 75mm pack howitzer with a shortened 105mm barrel placed on it. Range was limited to only four miles and this weapon became obsolete right after the war.

Below.
The M1 57mm anti-tank gun was assigned to the infantry regiment's anti-tank company. Although not as powerful as the troops might have wanted, it was a major improvement over the previous 37mm gun which it replaced in 1943. It could be used to fire high explosive shells against infantry, but was generally used in defensive positions against enemy tanks. Each infantry regiment had 18 of these guns.

23

Previous page, bottom.
Another staged shot showing troops training 'under all conditions'. Here a rifle team, with a light .30 caliber machine gun on the right, has been ferried across a river by an amphibious jeep. Some type of explosive has been detonated in the mud behind them to add to the dramatic effect. These troops do not wear their leggings for some reason.

Above.
This display of vehicles from the 13th Armored division provides a good comparison of sizes. From the left are two motorcycles, a 'seep' (an amphibious jeep), a 1/4 ton jeep, an M3 halftrack, an M3 Stuart light tank, an M4 Sherman, an M8 75mm howitzer carrier, an M3 armored car, and the gun motor carriage (a 3/4 ton truck with 37mm anti-tank gun mounted on it). The bumper marking for armored units used a triangle to indicate an armored unit so as not to confuse the letter 'A' with vehicles attached to an Army level unit.

Below.
Three MPs from a Negro unit are shown mounted on their Harley Davidson motorcycles. They wear the dark blue and white MP armband and Sam Browne leather belt with the standard four pocket service coat. It is interesting that they do not wear leggings or riding boots, and do not have 'MP' painted on their helmets. Note the sirens mounted above the headlights.

Above.
A July 1942 photograph showing the three most common uniforms of the Women's Auxiliary Army Corps. From left to right are the officer's winter uniform, the officer's tan cotton summer uniform and the enlisted woman's winter uniform. As the WAAC was not an official part of the Army, they had to use a different cap badge and buttons. The ugly eagle seen here on the winter officer's cap was known as 'the walking buzzard'. Once the WAAC was accepted into the Army in 1943 the buttons and cap badges were changed to the standard Army versions. The belt was dropped from the uniforms in September 1942.

Right.
Typical of the period is this shot of an Army nurse (note the collar insignia) able to keep up appearances in the field. It is doubtful that many nurses in an area where helmets were needed actually used lipstick and perfume sprayers, but images like this reassured the folks at home that women were kept safe from 'dangerous areas'. Bright red lipstick was commonly worn by most women of the time.

Late uniform regulations would show that the women were issued a wool knit glove insert, but this one has gone with her red fingernails and lipstick. She is wearing a special version of the M1 helmet. It is just a little bit smaller than the one worn by GIs. Also note the leather glove worn over the wool insert. This was one of the few leather items issued by the Army in a black color—previously, almost all leather was a brown color.

Above.
The Navy was able to attract women easier than the Army due in part to their better looking uniforms. Here is shown an Army nurse in blue uniform, a Navy nurse, Navy WAVE officer, and an Army WAAC officer with the 'Hobby' hat (named after the founder and commander of the WAACs- Oveta Culp Hobby).

Left.
The Army had a great deal of trouble designing good uniforms for the WACs. It was generally considered that the Navy and Marine female uniforms were much more stylish than the Army ones. One attempt to provide a good looking uniform was this beige off duty dress, worn here with branch of service collar disks and the female overseas cap. Brown shoes, gloves and purse complete the ensemble.

Below.
If you have swimming training you need lifeguards, and this is one more job that a woman can replace a man at. Needless to say if you have WAAC lifeguards you need a uniform for them, and this may be the only photograph taken of it. The patch is for Red Cross water safety instructors. These suits may have been locally made for the WAAC training center, as there is no record of any official WAAC swimsuit in the quartermaster catalogs.

Right.
There were eight of these M1917A1 water cooled machine guns issued to each heavy weapons company. The water in the barrel jacket kept the heat, built up from continuous firing, from warping the barrel. The black hose allowed steam to flow out and collect in a metal condensing can. Then the water could be reused in the gun again. Not only could this weapon be fired directly at a target, but the solid tripod allowed it to fire indirectly: raining bullets down on an unseen target plotted solely by map. The canvas ammunition belt shown here is white, but by 1943 all new belts were dyed the standard olive drab color.

Left.
Hot food was considered to be essential to morale and every squad was issued with one of these single burner gasoline M-1941 stoves. Originally a mountain troops item, it was transported in a cylindrical metal container, used here to hold the soldier's other mess gear. His M36 musette bag and other web gear hang from the tree behind him. The holes in the utensils slipped over the mess kit handle when the mess gear was dunked into boiling water for sterilization after use.

Left.
This Signal Corps sergeant is standing in front of three fluorescent ground panels generally used to signal aircraft. He wears an early pattern one piece HBT coverall, and carries the equipment of a telephone lineman, as well as an EE-8 field phone in its leather case. Regulations state that every soldier must wear some sort of headgear when outdoors, and this man wears only the helmet liner- a common practice when not in combat.

Crossing water was a constant problem in all theaters of war. A standard training exercise was to transport a 3,250 pound jeep across a stream without the use of a bridge. Here improvised floats are used to bring a jeep with a full load of ammunition (the black canisters in back) safely across chest deep water.

Right.
Slung on the back of this radio operator is the SCR-195. It was the first radio to be given the nickname 'walkie-talkie', as it was the first radio that one man could walk and talk into at the same time. He wears an American flag armband designed to show natives that invading troops were Americans. These armbands were used extensively in the Mediterranean, but not in the Normandy invasion. Under his left arm is the service gas mask bag.

Good field hygiene was continually promoted by the Army, and here we see the typical equipment carried by the GI. He is washing out of his steel helmet, with the liner conveniently placed to show off the interior. In front of him is arrayed his olive drab towel, black plastic soap holder, toothbrush, comb, shaving soap in a tube, shaving brush, and razor. This is all the equipment the Army felt a man needed to have to stay clean and fit in the field. A black plastic razor was issued to the troops, but it did not work well and was generally replaced by a higher quality razor purchased at the PX.

Above.
As part of an exercise off Camp Bradford Virginia, these LCS (Landing Craft, Support) lay down a smoke screen to hide the wave of landing craft in the background. Eventually it was decided that the use of smoke in landing operations caused just as much trouble to the troops trying to land in the right spot as to the defenders, so smoke was not frequently used in actual operations.

Right.
The LCVP (Landing Craft, Vehicle Personnel) capable of carrying up to 36 men, or a three ton vehicle. This was generally the first landing craft to hit the shore. It used a crew of three men and had a range of about 100 miles, but was prone to swamp in rough waters. It was carried on a larger transport ship then lowered into the water for the final run into the beaches. The coxswain, visible here behind his steering wheel, steered from a rather exposed position.

Below.
Members of the 'Scouts and Raiders' detachment train at Fort Pierce Florida in different sized rubber assault boats. The Scouts and Raiders were a little known unit trained to explore landing beaches and guide the first invasion waves into the correct location. In Normandy they were unfortunately assigned to man the rocket firing landing craft, and were unable to help direct the first waves to their appropriate sectors.

AMPHIBIOUS TRAINING

The LST (Landing Ship, Tank) was the largest of the vessels that could land vehicles and men right onto the beaches. Here can be seen the massive steel bow doors that open up to let the ramp down. Called 'Large Slow Targets' by their crew, they were one of the most important vessels used in the war. Considered ocean-going ships that could travel the world under their own power, they were armed with one 40mm (seen directly over the bow) and six 20mm guns.

Left.
The LST could carry up to 20 Sherman tanks, or 2,100 tons of other vehicles and men. Originally they were designed to drop an anchor off the stern when heading into the beach, then ram as far on shore as possible. Once their cargo had disembarked, a powerful winch would pull them back off the beach. In Normandy they were beached on the sand at high tide, then when the water receded the cargo could drive right off the ramp onto dry land.

US547

Right.
After practicing disembarking from the LST, this group of soldiers and sailors takes a break on the beach at Camp Bradford Virginia. Most wear the olive drab HBT fatigue uniform, with one sailor wearing the blue Navy work uniform.

34

Right.
Looking down into an LCM (Landing Craft, Mechanized) from a Navy transport ship. Note the distinctive perforated ramp of the LCM. Although the truck takes up most of the room, the crew has worked a trailer and a number of men into the odd corners. Clearly visible is the rope ladder the men had to climb down, as well as the twin .50 caliber machine guns. The truck would have been lowered by crane into the craft.

Below.
This front view of the an LCI shows the two ramps that the passengers would debark from. Because this small craft offered an inviting target of almost 200 men, it was generally used to bring in the follow up waves of troops, and not used in the initial landings. A 20mm gun is mounted right over the bow, and could be used to suppress any fire coming from the shore.

The LCI (Landing Craft, Infantry) had berths for 188 men below decks. It allowed an entire infantry company to land as a single unit without having to split the men up between different crafts. It was armed with four 20mm guns, and while the passengers may not always have a comfortable ride, at least they had a chance to stay warm and dry, (but crowded) before hitting the shore.

Top.
Experiments with other landing craft ended up with the LVT-4 (Landing Vehicle, Tracked). Due to problems in the Pacific with men being shot as they had to climb over the sides of similar vehicles, the Mk 4 version had a stern ramp for loading and unloading. There are 20 men visible either on or boarding this LVT-4.

Left.
Another variant of the tracked landing craft was the LVT(A)-1 (Landing Vehicle, Armored). This was essentially an amphibious tank with a Stuart turret (37mm gun and .30 caliber machine gun), and two 30. caliber machine guns on the rear deck. The Army had over 300 of these in operation by the end of the war.

Below.
The LVT-4 could also carry a jeep. 6,000 of these LVT's were obtained by the Army, and many of them saw action in Europe. 500 were shipped to the British under lend lease provisions. They proved very popular in the waterlogged areas of Holland, as well as the final river crossings in Germany.

This well staged shot in front of a transport plane shows how paratroopers wore their equipment when jumping. The M36 musette bag, generally slung between the legs under the T-5 reserve chest pack as seen here, is a post-1943 transitional model of dark OD#7 canvas and light shade trim. On his right hip he wears the folding carbine holster. On his left hip he wears the folding entrenching tool and an odd shaped bag that possibly held radio antennas or radar beacon equipment.

THE AIRBORNE TROOPS

Above.
The M-8 75mm pack howitzer was the only artillery that could be airdropped with the paratroops. It was broken down into seven different sections that were individually dropped. Rounding up all the different pieces, as well as ammunition containers, was quite a task for the airborne artillerymen. These men all wear the M42 jump uniform, and have the large service gas mask bag on their left side.

Previous page.
Against a backdrop of camouflaged parachute material, this Master Sergeant stands ready for action festooned with a wide variety of bags and equipment. His musette bag is slung between his legs, but the other bags could hold any manner of equipment. The two on either side are demolition bags, but airborne troops were known to use a variety of issue and locally made equipment to carry the tools of their trade. A 'Mae West' flotation vest is worn in case he lands in water. On his right hip he wears both a folding carbine holster and a machete.

Previous page, far left.
Standing in the door of a simulated aircraft, this paratrooper trainee wears the standard infantry combat boot (buckle boot) instead of the high lace up paratrooper boot. In 1944 the Army decided to issue this combat boot to all personnel, and make the paratrooper boot obsolete. When the paratroops became worried that parachute risers might catch in the boot straps, they were told to tape them up before each jump.

Right.
An excellent illustration of the paratrooper helmet chin straps as well as the harness and reserve chute bag clipped to the front. Barely visible on this soldier's left hip is a small canvas compass case. The white web static line is clipped to a wire running the length of the aircraft. When the paratrooper jumps from the plane, the static line automatically pulls out the parachute at a set distance from the aircraft. If it does not open, the trooper can manually pull the rip cord handle on his reserve chute. Note the hard metal seats with seat belts running along the side of the aircraft.

Right.
The message capsule is carefully placed on the leg of the pigeon, with the hopes that the bird will swiftly fly back to its coop at headquarters. Details of the baggy pockets with twin snaps of the M42 Paratrooper uniform are seen on the left. Just above the M1A1 Thompson can be seen the twin zippered area where all paratroops kept their emergency switchblade for cutting themselves loose from tangled cords.

Below.
Pigeons were considered a more reliable means of communication in the early days of radio. The birds were more rugged and survived the hard drops better than the sensitive electronics in the radios. These paratroops have taken a pigeon from its special airborne drop cage, and have attached a message to its leg prior to release. The Thompson machine gunner on the right carries the standard length of rope (33 feet) to use in case he needed to lower himself from a tree top landing

This paratrooper has camouflaged his jump uniform with splotches of different colored paint. This was commonly done among pathfinders, and in a few of the airborne companies. The cords on his shoulders are the risers that run from the harness to the parachute. The bag on his left side appears to be a camouflage painted demolition bag. His paratrooper helmet has a very wide and flat early production chin cup.

Above, and left.
These men are identifiable as officer cadets from the OCS patch worn on the lower sleeve. They are training in winter warfare conditions, and carrying the 1917 Enfield rifle. This bolt action rifle, although a perfectly good weapon, was often used for training when there were shortages of the M1 Garand. They wear the standard enlisted man's overcoat, which was considered too bulky for use in combat. The snowshoes are the standard trail variety normally used in areas where there was little vegetation to catch on their large size. These photos were taken in Wyoming.

Right.
This mountain trooper has the version of reversible parka with wolf fur trim around the face and cuffs. The gloves are non-standard and resemble the Air Force A-9 winter flying gloves. The white ski pole could be either the steel, or laminated cane version.

Below.
A bitterly cold scene possibly from one of the numerous Arctic weather food tests. These men wear a reversible parka tan side out, while contemplating cardboard boxes of rations. Their mountain rucksacks (one with ice axe attached) lie off to the left. The quartermaster corps continuously experimented with rations to make sure they were palatable under every condition and would provide enough nourishment even in the harshest climates. In some tests the ration designers themselves acted as guinea pigs to see if their food was edible in such cold conditions.

Previous page, bottom.
These mountain troops at Camp Hale have rigged a shelter from a two man mountain tent, supported by their skis and local branches. They eat from the standard mess gear, and have a 1903 Springfield rifle prominently displayed. One man per squad carried this rifle up through mid-1944 to fire rifle grenades from. Some soldiers preferred it over the M1 Garand for its greater accuracy. This photo provides a good look at the military ski binding.

Above.
A number of different uniforms are visible in this award ceremony for the Medal of Honor. This is obviously late in the war, as many of the men wear the short Ike jacket. A few enlisted men wear the leather garrison belt even though it was no longer authorized. Almost all the men here wear the Combat Infantryman's Badge, with the exception of two men with the Combat Medic's Badge, and the central tank officer (who not being in the infantry was ineligible for it). In the front row a paratrooper can be seen wearing his trousers bloused into his jump boots. He also wears his jump wings above his ribbons with the CIB below: this was against regulations but a common wartime practice for paratroopers.

Right.
Private William Soderman of the 9th Infantry Regiment, 2nd Infantry Division receives the Medal of Honor from President Harry Truman. Private Soderman was awarded the medal for his action near Rocherath, Belgium in December 1944. Three times he took out the lead German tank with a bazooka, thus stalling the German offensive. Underneath his Combat Infantryman's Badge, he wears only the Purple Heart and ETO ribbon. Curiously the Good Conduct ribbon is missing. Possibly this is an indication that poor soldiers make good fighters.

Below.
Private Mary Jane Ford was the first WAC to receive the Soldier's Medal for bravery. She risked her life to save a drowning man, and is being awarded the medal by General Ingles (the Chief Signal Officer) in July 1944. The other ribbons on her uniform are for the Good Conduct and WAC medals, indicating she had enlisted in the WAAC and then stayed on when it was incorporated into the US Army as the Woman's Army Corps. She wears the female version of the summer weight khaki wool uniform.

Right.
Trainees were kept up to date on the progress of the war. Up until the surrender of Germany, many of them had no idea if they would be sent to Europe or to the East. Here we see a group examining the latest news from the Pacific Theater (and probably hoping that things will be over before they get shipped out). All wear the HBT fatigues, except for the tech corporal (technician fifth grade) with the Replacement School Command patch, who wears the khaki cotton shirt and pants. He is probably allowed to wear this uniform as he is a member of the school staff.

Below.
The last stop before Europe- these troops carry all their belongings onto the transport that will bring them across the ocean. They carry full M1928 haversacks with the horseshoe blanket roll. This photo was taken late in the war, as they carry the duffel bag (standardized in April 1943) and not the earlier model barracks bag. By insisting that troops bring a complete set of uniforms and equipment with them (even their weapons), the quartermaster corps was able to free up a great deal of shipping space for other cargo.

Above.
Lieutenant General Mark Clark was the commander of the 5th Army. He was the principal American ground commander for the Italian Campaign. He is seen here with one of his WAC secretaries (a technician 4th grade) at a headquarters in Italy. Both wear the dark green scarf that was favored by 5th Army Headquarters personnel. The gold colored piping worn by General Officers is seen on Clark's cap. On his left hand can be seen the West Point ring: a status symbol for having attended the Academy.

Below.
The Medal of Honor is presented to Brigadier General William Wilber at the Casablanca Conference in January 1943. General Patton helps President Roosevelt with the medal, while George C. Marshall looks on. Wilber had been on Patton's staff during the invasion of North Africa. He volunteered to drive through potentially dangerous French lines to ask senior French officers not to fight the Americans. This action earned Wilber a promotion to Brigadier General and the MOH. Patton is seen here as a two star Major General wearing the patch of the 1st Armored Corps.

Opposite page.
A view of a large ship at Sicily shows the crew keeping a careful eye on an unknown aircraft. At this stage of the war, the German Luftwaffe was still a potential threat and the Navy took no chances. Some of these men wear the standard Army HBT fatigues. Since the man on the left has what appears to be USN stenciled on his back, they may be from the 1st or 2nd Beach Battalions (the Navy beachmaster unit in charge of the landing, but issued Army uniforms). The rubber rafts may be on hand for emergency use to rescue men in the water.

Above.
This 3/4 ton WC-51 Dodge truck at Salerno is from the anti-tank company of the 38th Infantry Regiment- 3rd Infantry Division. A similar vehicle can be seen behind it towing the 57mm anti-tank gun. The 3/4 ton Dodge was designed to haul the smaller but ineffective 37mm gun, and was quickly replaced by the larger 3 axle Dodge WC-62. On the front bumper can be seen an unusual tactical marking from the 3rd Division. In the rear can be seen LST-1 and the pontoon bridge with two LCMs (note the perforated ramp tops) moored to it.

Left.
Before Italy could be invaded, the island of Sicily was needed as a logistical base. The Sicily landings were better executed than the previous invasion of North Africa. This is an excellent overhead view of an American LCVP with supplies being lowered in a cargo net. Visible in the rear of the boat are the twin machine gun positions, although the coxswain's steering gear is lost in the shadow. The Navy crewmen wear a wide assortment of uniform items, but interestingly enough have helmets painted in the standard OD color- not the navy blue-gray.

Above.
The Navy cleverly solved the problem of landing troops and vehicles in shallow water by bringing 175 foot pontoon bridge sections with them. They attached these pontoons to the sides of LST's. Then, once at the landing beach, dropped them in the sea and used them to form a floating bridge from the sand to the deeper water. This technique was possible in the Mediterranean because of the calm ocean, but would not be possible in the rougher waters off Normandy. Interesting notes about the soldiers are the wearing of both white and OD undershirts, and that a medic can be seen wearing a Red Cross armband but no helmet markings.

Below.
This beach scene could be at almost any invasion site, but is believed to be at Salerno. The orange marker indicates which beach this is to the landing craft crews. The trucks in the background have oversized national star markings on their doors. The infantrymen coming across the beach wear the standard wool uniform with leggings and M1928 pack. They wear no field jackets due to the warm weather.

Above.
Members of either the 1st, 2nd, or 4th Navy Beach Battalion at Anzio display a variety of souvenir pistols they have picked up. It was common knowledge that ship's crews would trade or pay for any captured weapons, and the Beach Battalions were in a unique position to play the middleman between the GIs and the sailors. Beach Battalions were Navy personnel under command of the Army, and were issued with Army uniforms. Seen here are both Navy blue working uniforms, as well as Army wool and HBT items and the wool knit cap commonly referred to as a 'Beanie' or 'Jeep' cap. In the background can be seen some of the sandbagged bunkers the men lived in.

Right.
The Anzio landings permitted the capture of a port area which allowed the LSTs to discharge their cargo right into the city. LST 394 provides a good view of the upper deck with a few trucks still waiting to be unloaded. The problem with the port at Anzio was that Germans held the high ground outside the city and could bring artillery fire onto most sections of the port and town. The rubble and destroyed buildings seen here are probably from German attempts to hit the ships.

Below.
The danger of the German artillery at Anzio was lessened by splitting the cargo up into smaller loads and landing them in the Dukw's seen here. As one Dukw brings a load of boxes onto the shore, a second in the background can be seen heading back out to a ship waiting in the harbor. Speed of unloading was critical, as the both the German artillery and Luftwaffe was a danger to waiting vessels. The burned out hulks of at least two ships can be seen in this photo. Also of interest is the camouflage scheme painted on the British truck parked by the rubble.

Right.
Germans captured at Anzio are issued with rations for their trip away from the beachhead. This man from the Luftwaffe may be a paratrooper as indicated by his high lace up boots. He's being given a meal of two cans of C rations. One can is either meat & beans, meat & vegetable hash, or meat & vegetable stew. The other can is the bread unit composed of crackers, coffee, sugar, and chocolate. Each box holds 24 full meals of 48 cans. The Americans wear the M41 field jacket, which would prove too thin for the cold Italian winters.

Below.
The bright sunshine of Italy (in the summer) was just what was needed for the slow speed of Kodachrome film. Here a movie cameraman takes advantage of the light to shoot from on top of his jeep. The jeep, although covered with dust, has chains on the tires to give added traction in the slippery mud. The cameraman has managed to obtain a pair of the highly coveted paratrooper boots, which were in demand as they not only looked sharp, but allowed the soldiers to do away with the cumbersome leggings.

Above.
Unlike the swift advance across France, the fighting in Italy was a slow uphill struggle, and the high command established a number of rest centers to give the men a break from the front line. Many of the soldiers in the 5th Army were able to get some time off to see the sights or just get out away from the front line for a few days. These happy men wear the standard wool trousers and shirt. The first soldier wears the newly issued combat boot (also known as the buckle boot) which replaced the old short boot and legging. Although a major step forward in footgear, this boot was not waterproof enough for the mud and rain of Italy. A patch from the 34th division is worn by one man. Since clothing was worn to shreds on the front lines, then new items issued, his companions could be from the same unit but just not had time to sew a patch on yet.

Left.
Once the Allies had landed, the Italians gave up their quest for glory and stopped fighting. This monument to Italians killed in the line of duty is used as a temporary pole for telephone lines. The sightseers in the jeep wear the khaki cotton uniform favored in the rear echelons.

Above.
The mine detector could only locate metal mines, so when the Germans started using wooden, glass and plastic mines the engineers would have to search by hand. Probing the ground with a bayonet or straight wire was the best way to make sure an area was really clear of land mines. The sections that have been cleared are marked off with white engineer tape. On the left a man is holding a roll of tape ready to extend the markings as the group progresses forward.

Below.
The slow defensive warfare fought by the German troops allowed for effective use of land mines. This SCR-625 was the standard mine detector used by the Americans in the war. Its effectiveness was severely hampered by the high mineral content of the Italian soil. The assistant is on hand to mark any mines that may be found for later removal. He carries the older bayonet, since the length allows for better probing into the earth. Both men wear the combat boot, as well as the winter combat jacket (commonly referred to as the tanker's jacket).

Above.
The wooden Shu-mine was one of the most commonly used non-metallic mines. It held just enough explosive to blow off a mans foot, but could not be located by the mine detector because the case was wood and the fuse was plastic. It was small enough to be missed when probing by hand and accounted for a lot of casualties by engineers clearing mined areas. When pressure was placed on the top section, it pushed the safety pin out of the fuse (seen here in the center of the box) and triggered the explosion.

Above.
This poor fellow from the 1st Armored Division has made himself very comfortable in a house constructed from ammo crates. Stenciled information on 105mm shells can be seen by the top of the axe. A gasoline can has been rigged over the door to provide a gravity feed of fuel to a stove- which has a chimney made from old shell cases on the right. He wears the M1943 field jacket and trousers with shoe-pacs. Under the jacket can be seen the high necked sweater that was designed to be worn under the M43 jacket as an additional layer. The green bottle is the standard beer bottle used in this time period.

Right.
One of the most effective tools of the war was the bulldozer- known to the Army as a 'Tractor, earth moving crawler'. The Army had not even begun to use mechanized earth moving equipment until late in the 1930's, but once the war started the engineers could not have done half of their work without this useful vehicle. Some versions had an armored cab to protect the driver. The Italian countryside seemed to move back and forth between the two extremes of mud and dust. Tracked vehicles like this were needed to stay moving in the thick mud.

Left.
When the rain fell, it came down in buckets. Obviously this soldier is not too pleased with what has happened to his slit trench which he probably labored long and hard digging the day before. He wears the shoe-pac, a boot with a rubber bottom and a heavily greased upper section. This boot was the answer to the leakiness of the combat boot, but was made with no arch support so it was hard on the feet when marching. Troops in Italy tended to get the first shipments of newly designed cold and wet weather uniforms, such as the shoe-pac, due to the harsh terrain and weather.

Above.
A typical scene of the advance up the Italian peninsula. These men carry such little equipment that they are probably engineers, with a truck just behind the photographer, instead of infantry. One man carries an SCR-625 mine detector, while a group of medics stand by on the right. The last man in line is also a medic, but carries a variety of bags instead of the standard wide suspenders with two medical bags.

Right.
There is nothing worse for the infantry than to be shelled while in a forest. The trees cause the artillery shells to burst in the air and scatter shrapnel everywhere- including straight down into foxholes and trenches. This photo shows the aftermath of light artillery fire in a wooded area. This forest in the Gothic Line has been stripped of branches and the trees are splintered up and the down the trunks. Had the artillery fire lasted longer, there would have been nothing left standing.

Above.
These Shermans from the 752nd Tank Battalion have been converted to hold the M17 rocket launchers with twenty 7.2 inch rockets. Tank number 34 in the front has its number painted not only on the rear left fender, but also in large yellow letters on the rear of the turret. This assisted identification by the command tank when all the other markings were covered with dust. A camouflage pattern resembling the British design can be clearly seen on this tank. The crewman on the rear deck wears his armored triangle patch over his heart- a tradition started by George Patton which spread to many armored units.

Below.
These halftracks from the 1st Armored Division, like most vehicles in Italy, are covered with a thick layer of dust. The unit must be in a safe area, as the machine guns still have their canvas covers on. Four cans of gasoline (screw on caps) are stored behind the front bumper, while a can of water (with the flip top) sits by the driver's compartment. The vehicles are parked a safe distance apart in case of artillery or air strikes.

Below right.
A Sherman tank from the 752nd Tank Battalion near Pisa Italy. The dust of Italy, which rapidly turned to mud when it rained, can be seen as the predominate color of this vehicle. The crew is wearing the typical wool shirt (as the nights grew cold) and the tanker's helmet. The jar on the fender might be filled with olive oil, but could possibly be wine for use when the crew felt there was no safe drinking water. Barely visible on the front glacis plate is the marking: 5A- 752. This indicates that the 752nd was attached directly to the 5th Army and not to an armored division.

Right.

This chow line shows a wide assortment of uniforms being worn by members of the 791st Ordnance light maintenance company (91st Division). The first man in line wears rubber overshoes, wool trousers, and the M43 field jacket. The other men wear either the M43 jacket or HBT fatigues. A clue to what's under the overshoes is the combat boots worn by the man with HBT cap. Overshoes were necessary with the combat (buckle) boots, as the seems leaked. Note the shattered windshield on the mud-spattered truck.

Below.

These showers are run by the 818th Quartermaster Sterilization Unit. The sterilization companies were developed to fight the spread of body lice. This unit would operate with a laundry company and a salvage repair company to form a salvage repair battalion. The troops would undress in this tent, put their personal items in a small bag, and clean up in the shower tent. Then they would receive a fresh, but different uniform. The laundry company would pick up the dirty clothes and wash them. The salvage repair company would sort and repair the washed clothes and issue them to the next group of men that came through. A good system, but the troops did not like always getting different uniforms that might have shrunk. The 818th would have come under the 5th Army command, and not be assigned to just one division.

Right.

Other men from the 791st Ordnance check out the facts about the latest rumors circulating, while they wait in line for chow. On the left, a soldier wears the high necked sweater, HBT pants, and combat boots, while on the far right the technical sergeant has the winter combat jacket (tanker's) with the knitted cuffs, and paratrooper boots. He also wears only the helmet liner as a hat- this was frequently done in non- combat areas. The photo was captioned that it was taken in Bologna Italy.

Left.
This convoy is crossing a ford in a shelled out Italian village. The crossing area has been well marked by white engineer tape indicating the area that has been checked for mines. The unit markings on the jeeps are just blurred enough that they cannot be made out, but it is interesting to note that neither of the last two jeeps has their 5 gallon gasoline can strapped in its holder. All the windshields are down and covered by the issue canvas cover, as required in a combat zone.

Opposite page.
This truck from the 1206th Engineers has replaced the winch with a water pump, turning it into a fire truck. It is interesting that only the very front of the truck has been painted red, while the rest is still OD. The abbreviation E.C.S. stands for Engineer Composite Section. This is just one of any number of small detachments given special assignments. They appear to be the firemen responsible for Lidi Di Camio, Italy

Right.
This photo could have been taken almost anywhere in Italy. The men are spread out on either side of the road and carry only the barest of essentials. The M1928 haversack was not liked by the troops, and many of them resorted to rolling up their possessions in a shelter half, then slinging it over one shoulder by a tent rope. This was known as a 'hobo roll'. It let the troops carry what they needed, but was easy to drop in a hurry when they came under fire. Even in the warm weather of Italy the combat troops wore the wool uniforms. It was easier to sweat a little in the day, when you needed the wool to stay warm in the cooler nights.

Left.
These men from the 85th Infantry Division don't seem too happy, which is surprising considering the Army preferred men in publicity photographs to at least seem content. The two men on the right wear the M43 jacket with button attached hood, while the man on the left wears the M43 jacket liner. This liner, with the distinctive large buttons, was supposed to be worn underneath the M43 jacket, but was frequently used as an outer garment. All men wear shoe pacs and have only the helmet liner on their heads.

Above.
This group of GI's seems very happy to be out of combat and on their way to a rest center. The clean uniforms are a good indication that they have already been cleaned up at a sterilization unit's shower. The men wear either the overseas cap or their steel helmet (some with red crosses).

Above.
Clean water was extremely important, so specialized engineer units were developed to provide a safe source of drinking water. Here a member of the 363rd Infantry Regiment Cannon Company fills 5 gallon water cans to bring back to his unit. They can be told from gasoline cans by their flip, rather than screw top. Clean water, stored here in portable canvas containers, was essential to keeping the troops from getting sick. There were strong regulations about drinking from untested water sources.

Right.
An army with the best radios in the world still found room for pigeons. This 3/4 ton Dodge truck has specially designed pigeon cages in the back. When batteries in the radios failed and telephone lines were cut, the pigeons could (nearly) always get through for emergency communications. Even though this truck has four wheel drive, it has snow chains on each wheel for added traction in the mud.
Just to the left of the pigeon handler's foot is the spare tire carrier- with the tire removed. This may have been due to a shortage in tires, but the design of this truck made it difficult for the driver to squeeze out past the spare and they frequently removed it for extra comfort.

Left.
This similar team is the British
counterpart to the American
air controllers. This photo
may have been taken just
next to the previous one, as in
the foreground there is an
American helmet. In the close
confines of Italy, British and
American specialists such as
these had to work closely
together. Creature comforts
have not been neglected-
notice the thermos in the
foreground, the cigarettes and
matches on the field
telephone, and the cardboard
rations box.

Left.
Archbishop Spellman, the Military Vicar of the US Army, visited Italy in 1944, and is seen here with Catholic chaplains from many different units. Most appear to be captains, and their uniforms are split between wool and cotton khaki. At the lower right a chaplain's collar insignia is clearly visible, as is the patch of the 91st Infantry Division.

ARMY CHAPLAINS

Right.
Great interest was shown in religious matters due to the closeness of the Pope. Here General Mark Clark, his chief of staff Major General Gruenther, and Monsignor Carrol pay a visit to Vatican City. Both officers wear the dark green scarf seen on 5th Army headquarters personnel. The driver has a red scarf, and has a red band painted around his helmet. This indicated an MP in a unit assigned to Army level (in this case the 5th Army). Although someone has tried to clean the jeep, it still shows dust in all the corners. On the fender is the gray decontamination unit. This is designed to spray a neutralizing chemical if the enemy used chemical weapons.

Left.
Archbishop Spellman said Mass for a few different units while on this trip, and here we see him providing for men from the 85th Division. The helmet liner visible at the bottom of the photo shows the divisional insignia (along with a mysterious yellow line). The men are devoid of any unit patches, possibly due to a recent shower and exchange of clothing in preparation for the visit.

Above.
The most interesting unit sent to Italy was the Brazilian Expeditionary Force. This photo shows four generals in various Brazilian uniforms. The Americans had to completely reequip the Brazilians with everything from uniforms to weapons, and provide training in how to use the new equipment. Once the American uniforms were issued, the Brazilian ones were put away until the return home.

ALLIES IN ITALY

Right.
Italy seemed to be the place where every army sent their extra troops. There were more nationalities present in the Italian Front than in any other area. Soldiers got used to seeing curiosities such as this Sikh MP from the 8th Indian Division.

Left.
This group of Brazilian soldiers are being trained in the use of the M1A1 bazooka. All of their equipment is standard US Army, but they still wear their lightweight Brazilian uniforms. A few Brazilian NCO chevrons can be seen. The Brazilian Expeditionary Force (known as the F.A.B.) is a controversial unit. Some historians feel that the amount of equipment and training they needed did not equal their battlefield accomplishments. However, one consideration is that the Allies wanted to develop a strong Brazilian Army to counterbalance pro-German Argentina. When the FAB returned home, they were the most powerful and well trained army in South America (and strongly pro-American).

Left.
This 92nd Division signal team is checking the phone lines that run past a series of German pillboxes. On the right the lineman wears his 92nd patch on an M43 jacket, along with wool trousers and shoe-pacs. He has the typical leather lineman's case, containing knife and pliers, on his belt. His partner, keeping careful watch with an M1 carbine, wears the service shoes with leggings.

Above.
General George C. Marshall on an inspection tour of Italy visits Colonel Ray Sherman, the commander of the 370th Combat Team. A combat team was the term used when a standard infantry regiment was strengthened with additional elements directly under regimental command. The 370th was one element of the Negro 92nd Infantry Division. The 92nd had a checkered career in Italy, but the official blame was always placed on the enlisted men and junior officers, not on the senior (White) officers.

Left.
Here a member of the 92nd Division headquarters company writes home while his companion keeps an eye out for enemy planes. The crisp new M43 jacket and clean wool trousers is a good indication of a headquarters unit in any army. The 2nd pup tent has a home built chimney extending from it, and the tent is composed of both an old tan colored shelter half, and newer dark OD shelter half.

Above.
An infantry unit from the 92nd Division advances past a knocked out German Tiger tank on the way to the Arno River. Captioned as being taken on 1 September 1944, these men are labeled as being from the 370th Infantry Regiment. By photographing them by the tank the photo implies that they destroyed it, although this was not necessarily the case. Common among all infantry units around the world were these two columns strung out along each side of the road. The men knew that if they bunched up they would present a better target and possibly draw fire.

Below, left.
In Viareggio Italy these men from the 92nd Division are welcome at this 'Service Club for Enlisted Men.' This is obviously a staged shot of men relaxing with their copies of Yank magazine, as the Italian Staff and some Negro MPs have come out to watch the photography session. The 92nd got more coverage than other units in Italy because even in 1944 it was still considered an experiment to allow Negro troops in combat. The Army wanted to show the folks at home how well it was working out, and how well they were being treated.

Below, right.
This member of the 92nd Division looks at a sign for the divisional rest center. On the sign is the Division insignia of a buffalo. This came from the term' Buffalo Soldiers' which the Indians had given to Negro soldiers in the American west. The Indians had never seen men like them before, and thought their hair looked like buffalo fur. Barely visible on the sign is the word "officer's" indicating that the Astor Hotel was a rest center for officers only. The majority of the officers in the 92nd were white, but the gap between officer and enlisted man was just as bad as any racial difference.

Left.
General Mark Clark (who never went anywhere without a photographer) awards the Presidential Unit Citation streamer to the company guidons of the 100th Infantry Battalion. This unit was formed from troops of Hawaiian and Japanese ancestry, and is considered one of the most decorated units of WW2. It was so successful that in August 1944 the 100th battalion became a part of the 442nd Infantry: a full regiment of Nisei (Americans of Japanese ancestry).

Right.
A typical Nisei of the 100th Battalion stands ready with his Garand and two grenades. Unlike what is seen in the movies, GIs were very careful when dealing with grenades. No one wanted to accidentally set one off. Experienced soldiers would tape the handle down, as seen here, as a precaution against the ring becoming snagged and pulling out the pin. The left hand grenade is secured with yellow tape, but is also tied to his M36 suspenders with string. The grenade on the right has had the spoon (the handle) slipped through the suspender ring, and then fastened with an elastic band.

Above.
Major General Charles Ryder was the commander of the 34th Infantry Division (the Red Bulls) in Italy. He took the 100th Battalion when other units were suspicious of a battalion of 'Japs'. He never regretted having this superb combat unit under his command, as they made quite a record for themselves. What looks like an armored plate, is more likely a wind screen to help keep some of the dust out of the jeep. Dust is everywhere, even on the General's .45 holster. He has the divisional insignia painted on his helmet, with two stars on either side of the red bull.

Top right.
This Nisei has constructed a fighting position from sandbags and the black cardboard tubes that artillery rounds were shipped in. The tubes would be filled with dirt, and the layering effect would absorb a lot of an explosion's power. The tubes provide good overhead cover for artillery air bursts, or from an enemy shooting down from a mountain (which was often the case in Italy). He is armed with the M1 carbine.

Right.
Staff Sergeant Masaru Suehire, from Honolulu, was awarded the distinguished Service Cross for his heroism in Italy. He wears no rank insignia, but does have his 34th Division patch on his left shoulder. He is armed with the M1928 Thompson sub-machine gun, identified by the distinctive finned barrel. They are obviously well behind the lines as there is no magazine in the gun. The sergeant has managed to obtain a pair of the highly coveted paratrooper boots for himself.

Above.
This first aid post of the 10th Mountain Division is typical of a battalion aid station. The wounded have been stabilized and are awaiting transportation to a medical facility further away from the front lines. The medic in the doorway wears the distinctive mountain trousers worn by both this Division and the First Special Service Force. Even though the weather appears warm, the blankets are needed to keep the wounded from going into shock due to loss of blood.

Left.
This medical jeep is marked to the 34th Division- 100th Battalion medical section. Metal struts have been added to it for holding stretchers. There were a number of different methods for carrying stretchers on jeeps. It was not until late in the war that the Army realized that a jeep could get much closer to the front lines than the larger ambulance, and began to officialy use jeeps in this way. The yellow disk on the grill indicates what class of bridge the jeep was able to cross (due to weight). Most of these bridge markers were made from painted coffee can lids.

Above.
This view clearly shows the 10th mountain Division patch on a medic with the small circular red cross markings. It made sense to have smaller markings for troops in the front lines. Even though the red cross was supposed to provide protection, medics still wanted to call as little attention to themselves as possible. Some of the other medics have painted their rank stripes on their helmets. This was a habit in some units, but not universally done. The aid station is located on the reverse slope of a hill to keep it safe from observation and artillery fire.

Right.
Probably taken at the same 10th Mountain aid station, this close up shows medics at work. The red crosses painted on their helmets are interesting. One pattern, the square, is unusual and appears to be distinctive to men from the 10th. The medic in front has a smaller circular design which may indicate he is from another unit- possibly a front line company aid man helping out. There was little standardization in painting helmets, and it seems to have been done on a unit level by whoever was considered the best artist (or was on the sergeant's duty list).

Above.
The artillery forward observer was vitally important to bringing accurate artillery fire on enemy positions. This observer is relaying messages between a field telephone in his left hand, and a radio in his right. The box beside him is the RM-29 relay, which allowed for radio equipment to be operated from a distance or to be tied into a field telephone network. Obviously this location has been in use for a while as there is pile of used K ration boxes in the upper left hand corner.

Below.
If the original captions are to be believed, these men are taking the reports of the above forward observer and plotting the information on their firing board. They will evaluate all the facts and make the decision which targets need to be fired at first. Unlike the German Army where one observer controlled just one artillery unit, the American system provided for greater flexibility. One American observer could potentially control all artillery units in his division, and corps. A raincoat has been thrown over the windshield to prevent reflections from giving away the jeep.

Right.
These German POWs were captured by elements of the IVth US Corps. This was probably late in the war, as a few men in the center wear the short M44 tunic. The various shades of field grey uniforms are more likely from production differences than from normal fading. None of the Germans in this photograph wear any decorations. Either they removed everything beforehand or the guards were sure to get as many souvenirs as possible.

Bottom.
This camouflage painted building, in the Viareggio area, was probably some official military installation. How much protection the paint scheme provided is unclear, but it appears to be pockmarked from some small arms fire. Even the windows are painted in a camouflage pattern.

Right.
Marlene Dietrich risked more than any other American performer to entertain the troops. As she had been born in Germany, if she had been captured she would have been in a great deal of trouble. Here we see her on a May, 1944 trip to sing for wounded soldiers. The men seem to be more interested in how she looks than how she sounds.

Left.
Payday on the hood of a jeep for men from the 3rd Infantry Division. The 3rd was one of the few units that normally painted their division insignia on the helmet. Under the watchful eye of a few MPs, an officer counts out Italian occupation money. On the fender of the jeep is the yellow colored gas casualty first aid kit.

Below.
Technical Sergeant Charles 'Machine Gun' Kelly earned his Medal of Honor while serving with the 36th Infantry Division in Italy. He earned a reputation as a one man army by slowing down a German advance. He fired two BARs until they jammed, then threw 60mm mortar rounds like grenades. To release the special safety used in mortar shells, he had to slam the round down on the ground to simulate the shock of firing, then toss it. The captain at the right wears the ribbons for the Silver Star, Purple Heart, American Defense, and ETO medals.

Above.
On the outskirts of an Italian town this burnt out Sherman stands guard over a body draped with a blanket. The tank has probably been here for a while, as indicated by the rust. Although an initial impression is that it is probably a crewman under the blanket, it is more likely a German soldier as American graves registration troops were very good about quickly removing bodies of US soldiers from roads and other highly visible areas. It is was considered very bad for morale to leave American bodies where fresh troops moving up would see them.

Right.
Major General John Sloan, commander of the 88th Infantry Division. His jeep has a vertical bar of metal welded onto the bumper. This served as a wire cutter in case anyone had strung a wire across the road. In combat areas jeeps traveled with the wind shield down, so that the glass would not reflect sunlight and call attention to the vehicle. It was also safer to drive with the glass down, as a stray bullet or rock thrown from a tank track could send shards of glass all over the jeep occupants. The General's jeep also has some additional horns added to the front grill so he can get through traffic.

This M2 floating treadway bridge was placed across the Po river in Northern Italy. This was one of the last natural boundaries before breaking out from Italy onto the Continent. Pontoon bridges that float on inflatable rubber rafts were not easy to use in Southern Italy, where heavy rains led to flash flooding. As soon as possible a more stable bridge was erected, but nothing could beat the time it took to get one of these pontoon bridges set up. The trucks are hauling engineer equipment, including assault boats.

Left.
A group of GIs in the khaki cotton shirt and trousers pose for this joke shot in Pisa Italy. The cotton uniform was worn in the hot Italian summer by non-combat troops. The garrison cap was made of matching material and was worn to follow the US Army regulations that stated that every soldier would always wear some sort of cover (headgear) when out of doors. Conversely, the cover must be removed when inside unless the soldier was under arms (carrying weapons)

Right.
This MP is guarding one of Mussolini's villas at Lake Garda. He is a member of the 150th MP company attached to the 15th Army Group. On his helmet is the insignia of the 15th Army and red band indicating that his unit is attached directly to an Army level headquarters. He wears the khaki cotton uniforms and has added yellow overseas stripes to his left sleeve- not regulation but very often done.

THE U.S. ARMY IN GREAT BRITAIN PREPARING FOR D-DAY

In Weymouth shortly before D Day, these troops from an Engineer Special Brigade (note the white arc on their helmets) board American LVCPs for the trip to a larger transport ship. In the background can be seen three silver barrage balloons. This photo was taken from one of the twin gangways on an LCI; the handrails are just visible in the foreground. At left is the bow of an additional LCI.

Above.
In the summer of 1941 America sent troops to garrison Iceland. This kept the island out of German hands, and freed up British soldiers for other duties. In May 1943 Lt. General Frank Andrews of the Army Air Force was killed there in a plane crash. His remains, along with 14 others, were buried with full honors in a cemetery on Iceland. The honor guard wears the standard enlisted wool overcoat and garrison cap. The light blue piping of infantry troops is visible on some of these caps. The men also wear the black necktie which was being phased out of service, but obviously was still in use in this' back water' location.

Left.
WACs were sent to England to take over a variety of non-combat jobs thus freeing men up to fight. A WAC could fill an office job just as good as, and in many cases better than, an enlisted man. These WACs wear the enlisted wool overcoat which would later be replaced by a lined poplin overcoat. The buttons are made from OD plastic to conserve brass, which was vitally needed for making ammunition. One WAC wears the standard brown leather gloves, while the other has black gloves. Shortages of clothing items for WACs forced the Army to overlook minor discrepancies like this. The bicycles were a very handy way to get around England where gasoline was heavily rationed.

This first-aid post in England has a number of unusual details. It is well camouflaged with a net over the roof and the large white spaces on the signs have been darkened to lessen visibility. A British bag with red cross marking sits on the ground. The green cross of the Pro Station indicates that any soldier may receive prophylactic treatment for venereal disease here. Realizing that there was no way to stop men from seeking female companionship, the Army tried to keep the VD rates down by providing extensive preventative care. A man who developed VD was in trouble only if he could not prove he had stopped at a Pro Station after possibly becoming infected.

Above.
When possible, casualties were evacuated by air to better equipped hospitals far from the fighting. Here wounded soldiers are being transferred from an ambulance to a C-47. The women in blue are flight nurses who were specially trained in taking care of

casualties while they were in aircraft. The special flight nurse flying wings can be seen on one nurse, while the 9th Air Force patch is visible on one of the crewmen. The lieutenant in the leather jacket wears the M4 lightweight gas mask bag.

Opposite page.
This classic photo of a paratrooper shows a man from the 101st Airborne Division ready to jump with rifle and bazooka. The rifle is broken down into its components and stored in the rectangular Griswold bag strapped diagonally across his chest. Also worn on the chest are the 'Mae West' inflatable vest, the reserve parachute, and the M36 musette bag. His knees have been reinforced with heavy canvas as was typical of many paratrooper uniforms worn in Normandy. He has the M1A1 bazooka, with muzzle covers, slung over his left shoulder.

Left.
The C-47 transport plane was used for hauling all kinds of supplies and equipment as well. Here a jeep is being driven up a ramp into the aircraft. The crew wears the patch of the 9th Air Force. The jeep has a container in the back for radio equipment and the antenna base is covered with a special black rubber bag. This was taken in England, probably in training, as the jeep has white stripes painted on the fenders and rear bumperettes. This was for increased visibility in the blackout conditions of wartime England, but would never have been found in combat. The shovel and axe normally strapped on the driver's side of the jeep are missing.

Above.
Medical technicians pack blood being shipped to hospitals throughout the ETO. Blood plasma could be transported in a dry state, stored indefinitely, and when re-hydrated given to anyone regardless of blood type. Whole blood, which still contained the red blood cells, would only stay good if continually refrigerated. It had be stored in dry ice and shipped by plane to the larger medical facilities. If a casualty was given only plasma (which was blood without the red blood cells) he could actually suffocate. The red cells carry oxygen around the body, and without them a man can gasp for breath but still turn blue and die.

Below.
This photograph was actually taken in California shortly after the war. It shows an inflatable rubber tank like the ones used to fool the Germans as to the location of American troops in England. By clustering large numbers of these inflatable dummies in certain areas, the Germans thought the invasion of France would come at Calais. The Allies made inflatable tanks, trucks, and even landing craft as part of this decoy operation.

Above.
LCT 495 is shown passing the British Navy trawler *Loch Park* during invasion rehearsals off the coast of England. The LCT is towing a barrage balloon which was designed to make it hard to attack the vessel by low flying aircraft. A plane trying to strafe the ship would be in danger of striking the heavy wire cable and crashing. When in a convoy or harbor, multiple balloons would be flown at various altitudes to make things ever harder for enemy pilots.

Below.
This unknown Army unit is shown on manoeuvres in a British country village. The men wear very little field equipment, and the first four men carry the M3 'grease gun' sub-machine gun. The M3 was developed to be cheaper and quicker to produce than the Thompson SMG. It was also issued to tank crews because its small size made it easy to manage in tight hatches. There are no real clues as to what unit this might be, but it remains a typical propaganda photo showing good relations between Yanks and Britons.

Right.
Technician 5th Class (Technical Corporal) Jack Bramkamp- the barber, and his client T/5 Elmer Olander, were members of Company B, 2nd Ranger Battalion. They were killed on D-Day before they even got off the beach.

Above.
Members of an Engineer Special Brigade kill some time while waiting to load their camouflage covered trucks onto transport ships. Their helmets have been painted with a white arc and the blue and yellow insignia of the Army Amphibious Engineers. The arc is believed to be a symbol showing that the wearer has a job to do on the beach and belongs there. Men without the arc would be driven off the beach by MPs. These engineers wear the paratrooper boots issued to the amphibious engineers (they were the only footwear that kept out sand while working in surf). All three have the black rubberized M5 assault gas mask bag, with one hanging on the truck. The left hand soldier carries a 1903 Springfield rifle which, due to a shortage of Garands, was issued to many replacements just prior to D-Day.

Opposite page.
Another view of Company B of the 2nd Ranger Battalion. On the ground is the special assault jacket issued to specific units taking part in the Normandy invasion. This canvas vest with many pockets was worn by the assault regiments, as well as the NCOs and officers of the Ranger Battalions. Tied to the assault jacket is the special parachutist first aid pouch which held a bandage, a tourniquet, and a vial of morphine. Next to it under the helmet can be seen the black rubber M5 assault gas mask bag. The man squatting down at center is holding a gray can of boot impregnation, which was applied just prior to the invasion as protection against possible chemical attack.

A signals section of the 7th Navy Beach Battalion sets up a communications point during a practice landing in England. They can be identified by the red 'USN-7' painted on their helmets. The 7th Beach Battalion would later be responsible for operations on the western side of Omaha beach-where the 29th Division would land. Here they are seen using the three main methods of communications: signal flags, blinker lights, and radio. The captain on the right wears an armband with the letter 'B' indicating he is a beachmaster-the man in charge of this section of the beach up to the high water mark. Although attached to the Army Amphibious Engineers for the Normandy landings, these men carry the Navy gas mask in the gray canvas case. All other equipment is of Army issue.

This photo of British LCA 1377 shows a lot of the detail of the front armor. A Ranger patch can be seen on the arm of one man- indicating these is part of the same series taken of Rangers boarding at Weymouth. It is interesting that a few of the helmets have red crosses painted on them. It is often debated if American medics at D-Day wore painted helmets, and here is proof that at least some of the medics assigned to the Rangers did so.

Above.
The last stop on shore for the Rangers was this tent with the sign 'check rosters here'. Transportation officers would double check the men against the official unit roster before letting them board the ship. Signal Corps movies taken at the same time show that coffee and doughnuts were handed out by the Red Cross on the other side of the tent. In the background can be seen the Weymouth Pavilion.

Below.
A diamond shaped Ranger patch can be seen on the shoulder of the lead man. Examination of these photos shows that some wore the patch, but many did not. This could be due to security precautions, or the fact that many Rangers disliked the diamond shaped patch because it resembled an American gasoline company sign. This close up clearly shows the black rubber M5 assault gas mask bag being

worn on the chest, and the American style inflatable life preserver worn around the waist. Many men were drowned at Normandy when this life belt slipped too low on their bodies, and the top heavy men were flipped upside down

The crew of a half-track 'somewhere in England' waiting their turn to sail for Normandy. The red color under the star on the hood is a special paint that changes color when exposed to chemical weapons like mustard gas. Exposure to heat and light would slowly turn it a reddish color. The tubing on the right side of the vehicle supplies air to the carburettor which helps water proof the engine for a beach landing. Barely visible on the 50 caliber ammo belt is a mixture of red and black painted tips of tracer and armor piercing rounds. The man on the hood reading a French language guide wears leggings that have obviously been cut down to a shorter size. This was commonly done by combat troops, as it made the leggings easier to get on or off. The camouflage net is woven with the standard two tone burlap strips found in Europe.

Top.
Behind the British LCA's can be seen American LCI's moored three deep at the pier. LCI 497 (at right) uses her port landing ramp as a gangplank. When it was time to load these ships the soldiers would board the LCI 497, and then climb over to their assigned ship (the LCI's 87 or 84). This illustrates the severe crowding found in the invasion ports.

Left.
Careful inspection of this photograph shows it to be men from the 2nd Ranger Battalion marching down the waterfront at Weymouth England ready to leave for Normandy. The Rangers boarded their ships on 1 June 1944, and spent the next 5 days stuck on British Transports unable to disembark for security reasons. Some Rangers can be seen carrying the 5 foot long bangalore torpedoes. All appear to wear the standard canvas leggings. Close inspection shows a few men wearing the dark colored assault jackets. Since these jackets were not issued until 10 days before the landings, the photo could not have been taken at an earlier practice invasion and must have been taken just prior to the real invasion.

Above.
These medics from an Engineer Special Brigade carry stretchers, but none of them have a red cross painted on their helmets. There had been rumors in Italy that Germans went out of their way to shoot medics, so some American units did not paint on the red cross markings. The men carry no weapons, but a few do wear the special medic's bags. A few of the stretchers have been tied to inflatable life belts so they will float in on the tide if lost at sea.

Right.
LCAs carry the Rangers out to their transport ships. These LCAs would then be hauled aboard ship and used for the final run in to the Normandy beaches. The LCAs were similar to the American LVCPs, but were more cramped due to their lightly armored sides and overhead protection. A number of British transport ships were used to land American troops at Normandy.

Above.
Port facilities were so crowded at the time, that the Rangers had to take British LCA (Landing Craft, Assault) out to their assigned transport ships. The fact that they boarded their ships five days before the invasion helped to fool any spies that may have been keeping an eye open for the movement of these elite troops. In the foreground a few men can be seen wearing the distinctive orange diamond shaped insignia painted on the back of their helmets. Only the 2nd and 5th Ranger battalions wore this marking. The vertical white bar was, by regulation, worn by all officers, and the horizontal white bar by all NCOs in the ETO.

Left, and opposite page, top.
These two close ups show Rangers in an LCA at Weymouth. A 60mm mortar can be seen on the overhead cover next to a conical mesh bazooka flash shield. A white pack of Lucky Strikes cigarettes is being handed around. The Lucky Strikes pack was originally green, but green dye was desperately needed for the military, so the company changed to white and got a lot of advertising mileage out of their slogan "Lucky Strikes have gone to war". The diamond shaped Ranger patch is worn on some of the M41 field jackets, and in one case can be seen in the upper right hand corner worn on the right shoulder. The men all wear their M5 assault gas mask bag on their chest, and the M1928 haversack is visible on a few of them. In the vertical photo the bazooka man carries a gray cardboard box, the box the lifebelts were issued in, which is covered with pencilled games of tic-tac-toe. At the top left can be seen a bangalore torpedo with a center hole on top designed to hold the detonator.

Opposite page, bottom.
An ambulance from the 1st Medical Battalion, 1st Infantry Division (note bumper markings), backs onto an LST. A red cross flag is furled on the right front fender. The yellow and black square seen on both the side door and bumper are believed to be a tactical marking for this unit. The large waterproofing intake tube can be seen on the right side of the ambulance, and the American flag waterproofing checklist is in the front window. The three horizontal stripes painted on the front bumper are a code specific to each company. These bar codes were supposed to be painted on all unit equipment and vehicles.

Above.
Troops of the 32nd Field Artillery, 1st Infantry Division, wait along a British country road on their way to embark for Normandy. The unit designation is just visible on the rear of the truck marked C-9 (ninth vehicle of battery C). The M2 105mm howitzers have been painted with the names of battles the 1st Division had fought in: 'Djebel Berda- Mt. Etna'. The next gun in front is marked 'Hill 407'.

Opposite page.
This MP is from the 1st Division Military Police Platoon. The yellow band on his helmet indicates he is from a divisional MP unit. A Springfield grenade launcher has been clamped to a thin metal tube on the windshield. This tube was part of the waterproofing system and vented the crankcase. The rifle is encased in a clear plastic bag to keep it dry in the landing. On the windshield is an American flag sign that served two purposes: first it identified the vehicle as American to the local population, and second it acted as the final waterproofing checklist for the vehicle. On the bottom of the flag is a space for the inspector's initials for both the vehicle and a trailer. The reverse side held reminders for de-waterproofing the vehicle once it was ashore.

Left.
This 105mm howitzer has been thoroughly waterproofed for its landing on Omaha beach. It is a gun from the 32nd Field Artillery, and has the battle names 'Troina and Oran' painted on the gun shield. The yellow rectangle also painted on the shield appears in the center of the white star of other 1st Division vehicles, and may be a tactical symbol for the unit (is the C for C Battery?). The crew has encased the breech block and other major components in a waterproof material of asbestos paste. All of this must be stripped away on the far shore before the gun will be ready to fire. The man on the gun has a painted 1st Division insignia on his helmet, which was normally worn by members of this division.

In the background, a truck containing a dismantled light observation plane is seen loading onto an LCM. These aircraft were used to spot targets for artillery units. Similar aircraft were launched off the decks of ships in the Mediterranean, this was not done at Normandy. The plane had to be reassembled in a Normandy field before it could be used. The ship in the background has covered her deck with camouflage netting. In front, a jeep from an Engineer Special Brigade is filled with a large load of equipment.

Below.
These MP's boarding an LCM in England have yellow helmet bands, but some show the edge of the white Engineer Special Brigade arc as well. The men all wear the paratrooper boot, so they are probably from an MP unit assigned to the amphibious engineers. Why their helmet band is yellow instead of white for a non-divisional MP unit is unknown. They carry their rifles in the clear waterproof bag and wear the standard M1928 haversack. Unlike assault troops who wore standard wool trousers at Normandy, these men wear HBT trousers. By special regulation for the Normandy invasion, these HBTs would be worn over the wool trousers for protection against chemical attacks.

Opposite page.
LST 357 is well known in photographs for its painted insignia of a stork with a baby and the slogan 'We deliver'. Here two Dukws are being backed onto the ship. These amphibious trucks can disembark off the ramp even when the ship is in deep water, land on the beach and drive inland to drop off their cargo at a supply dump. The 3/4 ton Dodge in the foreground has no unit markings on it, but is most likely assigned to the port staff as it has not been waterproofed and carries none of the extra equipment found on most vehicles heading for the continent.

Right.
An LCT loads up on the hard concrete ramp built specifically for troop embarkation. In the background two LSTs lie in deeper water taking on their load. . Due to their slow speed, some of the LCTs were the first to sail,and the last to return when the invasion was postponed due to bad weather. No sooner than they got back to the harbor, they set sail again for the 6 June landing. The men who were in these boats, predominantly from the Engineer Special Brigades, landed on D-Day after spending two days seasick in a small boat with no facilities for them.

Below.
This jeep is driven onto an LCT by a member of an Engineer Special Brigade. Although it has no red crosses painted on it, the flag indicates it carries medical supplies and personnel. The Engineer Special Brigades were actually logistical organizations that contained not only engineers, but every unit needed to run a major port- including medical support. The jeep has half canvas doors which helped prevent road dust and mud from getting in. The driver wears his wool knit cap with the brim to the rear. This was commonly done, but the knit hat was only supposed to be worn under the helmet, not by itself.

Below.
A Dodge WC-62 three axle weapons carrier tows a 57mm anti-tank gun from the anti-tank company of the 8th infantry Regiment, 4th Infantry Division. The unit markings are clearly visible in other photographs from this same series. The gun crew wears the M41 jacket, HBT trousers (over wool trousers), leggings, and M1928 haversack. They also carry a OD#7 dark shade M4 lightweight service gas mask bag. This is proof that some OD#7 dark shade webbing equipment had been issued to troops in England prior to the Normandy invasion. The sailors standing nearby wear the standard Navy work uniform of blue shirt and dungarees.

Above.
This half-track is armed with quad .50 caliber machine guns. It has been given the nickname 'Brass City' probably due to the large amount of fired brass shells the vehicle fills with when firing. A faint camouflage pattern can be seen painted on the side of it. This is unusual as most American vehicles were painted only in the standard olive drab. Every spare inch of space seems to be filled with extra supplies and crew possessions.

Below.
This front view of an LCT loading shows how crowded it got on these small ships. The jeep in front, named 'Bub', has a vertical metal beam welded to the front bumper to act as a wire cutter. Most other jeeps seen in these pre-Normandy photos do not yet have wire cutters. The half-track on the right is another anti-aircraft vehicle mounting .50 caliber machine guns. Painted on the front are the words 'Beach Defense'. This was probably to show that the vehicle had a reason to be on the beach, and should not be moved away by the MPs.

Opposite page.
This well known photograph shows a group of 1st Division GIs waiting to sail to Normandy. The divisional insignia has been painted on most of their helmets, and some of them (though not all) wear the shoulder patch. Everyone wears the standard wool trousers and either an M41 or winter combat jacket. From the lack of weapons and equipment this group is probably not from a combat unit, and due to the number of goggles seen they may be a group of vehicle drivers that would land in a later wave. Behind them a few cranes have been loaded as part of the amphibious engineer's equipment. The lone Negro soldier at right wears an HBT jacket. He is not from the 1st Division, but probably from one of the many support units of the Engineer Special Brigades.

This truck from an unknown 1st Infantry Division unit has another yellow tactical mark painted in the center of the white star. The name 'Chinn' painted on the hood and door is probably the name of the driver permanently assigned to the vehicle. It was standard practice in some units to paint the drivers name on the vehicle much like a pilot had his name on his aircraft. Other units gave every vehicle nicknames starting with the first letter of their company. On top of the cab is a .50 caliber machine gun in a canvas cover. These machine guns were mounted on vehicles to provide for anti-aircraft defense. Some of the sailors in the background are wearing red cross armbands. After the LST had unloaded in Normandy, the ship was expected to bring back a cargo of wounded GIs and POWs.

Above.
These Sherman tanks are from the 741st Tank Battalion as indicated by the markings on the trailer of the M4A1. The large sheet metal fording devices provided for the intake of fresh air, and the exhaust from the engine if the tank was dropped off in deep water. These intakes would be removed as soon as the tank was ashore. The American flag with waterproofing information is placed on the front of the second Sherman, an M4.

Left.
Looking across the loaded LCTs, soldiers are settling down for their ride to Normandy. Most of the men are putting on and adjusting their inflatable life belts. The two soldiers in the center foreground have camouflage painted helmets. There seems to be a mix of both the standard M41 field jacket, and the winter combat jacket with the knitted collar and cuffs. This jacket was warmer, more durable, and a highly sought after item.

105

One of the few color photos taken from the invasion area, this shot shows three men on either Utah or Omaha beach. One man wears the blue patch of the Army amphibious engineers which makes him a member of an Engineer Special Brigade. The two men in front wear paratrooper boots which were issued to that unit. The third man in the rear has a blue arc painted on his helmet which denotes an unknown element of one of the engineer brigades.

Most arcs in these units were white, while the 6th and 7th Navy Beach Battalions had red arcs. A possible clue is the white canvas bags that appear at the bottom of the photograph. These bags resemble some of the life preservers used at the time, but they also might be a special explosive known as the Hagensen pack. This consisted of two tubes of canvas filled with explosives and tied together with a short length of canvas. The other

ends of the tubes had a hook and eye attached so the pack could be easily wrapped around the steel girder of an obstacle and quickly secured. Hagensen packs were only used by the Navy Combat Demolition Units. Many photographs show that soldiers liked to sit on their explosives (showing a devil may care attitude), so the blue arc may refer to that unit. Off the coast is seen the massive fleet used to land the troops in France.

In August 1944 a second amphibious invasion of France took place in the Mediterranean. These men are some of the principal commanders of that operation. Left to right are: Brigadier General Saville, Major General Patch, Vice Admiral Hewitt, Secretary of the Navy James Forrestal, and Rear Admiral Lemonnier of the French Navy. This photo was taken on board the flagship *USS Catoctin.*

Below.
Also on board the *Catoctin,* men crowd around an impressive relief model of the invasion area. Some of these men may be the crews of the LVCPs seen hanging on the davits in the background. Three-dimensional maps such as this provide them with a greater understanding of the areas where they will soon be landing troops. Meticulous planning allowed the Southern France landing to go off without any major problems. At one point the landing craft heading to a heavily defended beach were diverted to an entirely different area. This tricky change of plan, in mid-operation, was accomplished only because everyone knew as much about the operation as possible. The Saint-Tropez peninsula is seen in the center of the map.

AUGUST 1944: OPERATION DRAGOON THE LANDINGS IN SOUTHERN FRANCE

Right.
The 1st Navy Beach Battalion command post shown here is on 'Alpha Red' beach near Cavalaire. This is the area where the 3rd Infantry Division landed. The two sailors on the right wear the HBT uniform, while the two central figures are probably Navy officers wearing the standard officer's khaki work uniform. One of the men they are conferring with wears the standard wool shirt and trousers (probably from the 3rd Division) while the other wears the HBT uniform (possibly an Army amphibious engineer).

Below.
With the town of Saint-Raphaël in the background, these LCTs and LCMs unload at 'Camel Red' beach. This area was under the control of the 8th Navy Beach Battalion and was the original landing site for the 36th Infantry Division. Due to the heavy defensive fire from Saint-Raphaël, the Regiment scheduled to land at 'Camel Red' was diverted to 'Camel Green' beach miles to the east. Saint-Raphaël was then captured from the rear. The 8th Beach Battalion set a record for landing the entire 36th Division over a single beach in one day.

Below.
A group of LCVPs tied up alongside a barge at 'Camel Red'. These unpowered barges were used to move material from deep water into the beach, but also to form an impromptu home port for the smaller landing craft. The white marker flags set up on the beach are used to help guide the boats through clear channels and in to the correct beach.

Above.
An M-15 half-track from the 441st Anti-Aircraft Battalion guards the area around 'Camel Red' beach. Its AA mount featured twin .50 MGs and a 37mm gun. Even though the German Luftwaffe could not operate in numbers in this area, transport ships made such an inviting target that these AAA units were needed. One LST was sunk nearby by a German radio controlled glider bomb.

Right.
Behind 'Camel Red' beach this German Mk II tank turret had been set up as a pill box to defend the beaches. A number of these obsolete turrets, armed with a 20mm and light machine gun, were found along the coastline, but they did not hold up the Allied advance.

Right.
As soon as the initial assault waves captured the beach, these Army engineers started to lay down sheets of wire mesh to form roadways. This kept the traffic moving over the loose sand without getting stuck. It was vitally important to get equipment off the beach as soon as possible, since the Germans knew the exact location of possible landing sites and would try to shell or bomb the area at all costs. An American flag armband is worn by some of these men. This armband was used only in the Mediterranean. It is not seen in any photographs from the Normandy landing.

Below.
'Beaufighter' is a Dukw from Company B, 52nd Quartermaster Battalion. This unit apparently gave nicknames to all vehicles. Each started with the same letter as the company they were assigned to (in company A one Dukw was called 'Anna'). This kind of official nicknaming helped identify what vehicle belonged to which company. The art work seen just under the machine gun ring shows a fighting duck which could be either a unit insignia, or just added by a talented crewman to this one Dukw. On the starboard bow is the typical three colored bar code that helped identify what unit this equipment belonged to. In theory all marks that identified anything larger than a company should have been erased for the invasion, but obviously this was not done by the 52nd QMC Bn. The machine gun was probably removed from its mount because the extra weight so high in the craft made it ride poorly in rough water.

Right.
More Dukws land at 'Camel Red' bringing supplies in from the transports anchored in deeper water. The ships would load a Dukw by lowering a cargo net filled with supplies into the Dukws hull. The Dukw would then swim to shore, drive out onto the beach as seen here, and head inland to a supply dump. It would drop its cargo and head back out to the sea for another load. By using an amphibious vehicle, the step of taking things off a landing craft and putting it on a truck was eliminated; thus drastically speeding up the process.

Above.
Enlisted German soldiers taken prisoner were put on LCTs, brought out to Liberty ships, and removed from the combat area. Many of these Germans seem to have suffered minor wounds. They all wear large cardboard tags giving information on where and when they were captured. The standard inflatable life belt has been issued to them for their voyage. Many of the Axis troops based in Southern France were not German, but conscripted from other countries. This explains why so many soldiers surrendered so quickly in this area.

Below.
According to regulations all officers must be kept separate from enlisted POWs. These German officers were captured in the first days of the invasion, and proudly displayed for the camera. Their decorations have probably already been liberated as souvenirs. The dark blue uniform in front was originally captioned as being for an air force officer, when in fact the man is an official from the German railway organization.

FROM NORMANDY TO THE REICH

Moving inland from the invasion beaches, the first breakout was to Brittany and the West of France. There was heavy fighting in the coastal town of Saint-Malo where this photo of a 60mm mortar squad (probably from the 83rd Division) was taken. Obviously posed,

the rubble made a good backdrop for these men. A 60mm mortar squad was composed of five men: a squad leader, a gunner, an assistant gunner, and two ammo bearers. The man crouching down in front has the brown leather mortar sight case on his belt.

Extra mortar ammunition is conspicuously missing. It may have been left out of sight along with field jackets and other equipment. The photo was probably taken around August 20, 1944.

Below.

A 57mm anti-tank gun, probably from the 83rd Infantry Division, looks out from Saint-Malo to the island forts of Petit Bey (left) and Grand Bey (right). The larger fort was taken by GIs from the 329th Infantry Regiment under cover of a smoke screen on 16 August, 1944. The 57mm gun may be watching for any activity on the islands, but this is probably a staged shot taken after the fighting had ended. The men preparing the shells do not seem to be too concerned with staying under cover. The gun crew is wearing the HBT fatigues, which look very new in color. The flag fixed to the gun shield is the same as used to show waterproofing in vehicle windshields. This marker has a place to list both the vehicle and anything it towed, so the flag was probably added by the crew as a decoration rather than because it was required by regulations. In the upper left corner of the gun shield can be seen a marking which is the unit serial number and the bar code used to mark organizational equipment.

A close up of the mortar crew in action shows the gunner aiming the mortar, and his assistant ready to drop a high explosive round down the tube. The M41 field jacket on the gunner is quite dirty, which may explain why the others would have taken them off for the photo. The mortar rounds are painted olive drab instead of the pre-war yellow. The round ready to enter the tube has the early aluminium fuse, while the round in the assistant gunner's right hand has the later black plastic fuse. This was developed to conserve metal. The man on the radio may not be from the mortar squad as he wears the HBT fatigues and carries an M1A1 Thompson.

Above.
This 60mm mortar crew is in a well-dug foxhole. By regulations a mortar emplacement was to be no larger than it took for the gun and two men. This meant less area for an enemy shell or grenade to land in. The round is a standard 60mm high explosive shell painted OD with the black plastic fuse. On the assistant gunner's helmet can be seen the letters 'AAAO' with a line drawn through them. This was the unofficial insignia of the 39th Infantry Regiment (9th Infantry Division) and stood for 'Anywhere, Anytime, Anyplace- Bar none'. This was frequently painted on helmets and equipment of men from the 39th. The slogan was resurrected temporarily by the unit when it later fought in Viet Nam. The photo caption says the men are from D Company, 39th Infantry.

Left.
The crew of a light anti-aircraft gun pass the time listening to a wind-up phonograph and reading *Life magazine.* The *Life* reader has acquired paratrooper boots, while his comrades wear the standard canvas leggings. By the end of 1944, the threat from German air attacks was at an end, and many anti-aircraft crews were given a quick refresher course and transferred to the infantry.

THE DESTRUCTION OF SAINT-LÔ

Saint-Lô was a key road junction in Normandy. The Germans defended it with great skill, and the Allies attacked the city with everything they had. The following six shots, taken on 35mm film, show the devastation of the city. These photos were taken after the Army had a chance to clear the roads of debris.

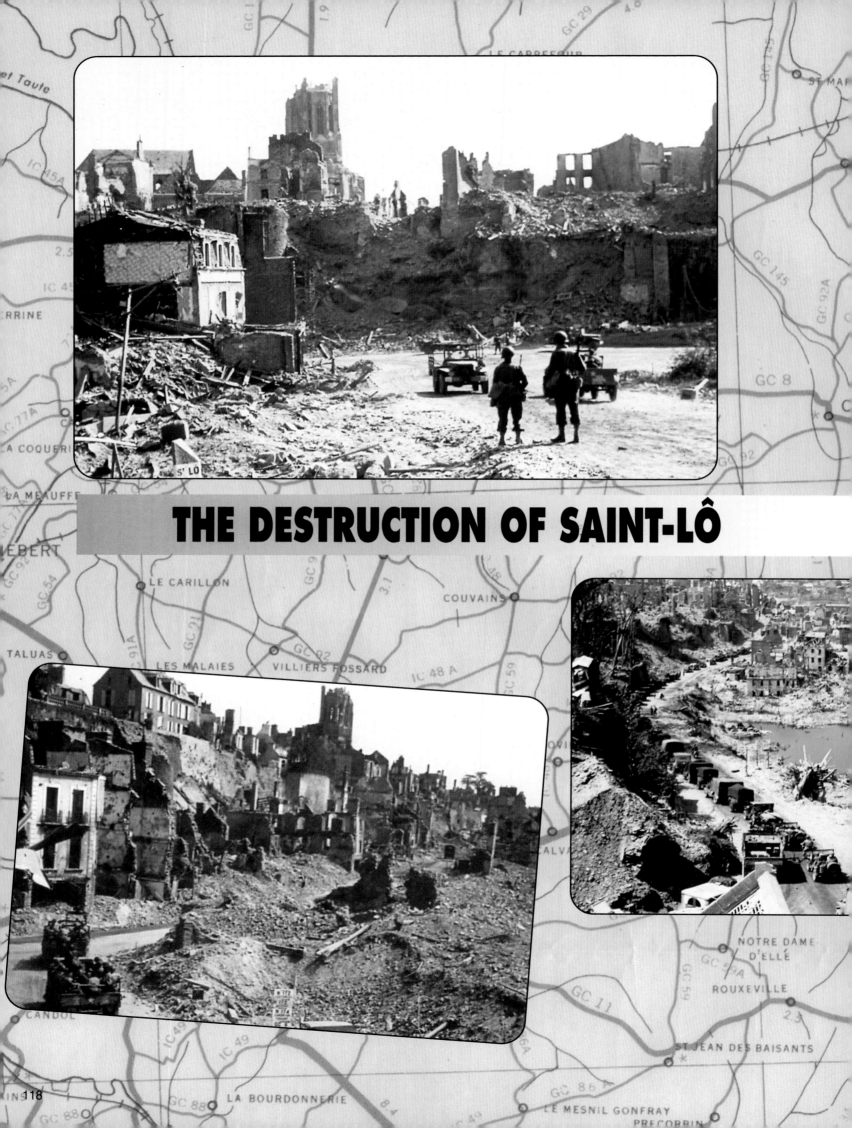

THE DESTRUCTION OF SAINT-LÔ

Above.
The bottom sign on the signpost points to 'Master Rear'. Master was the code name for the U.S. First Army. So 'Master Rear' stood for the Rear HQ of the 1st Army. These code names were developed to hide the identity of a unit in communications and on signs like this. Every unit down to a regiment or independent battalion had their own code name.

When the US Army moved into the old front line of WW1, some units found themselves on the same ground they had fought on in the Great War. Here men of the 75th Infantry Division take a moment to ponder a French Monument from the First World War battles on the Marne.

Below.
Whenever the infantry had a chance to pull out of the front lines, they were sent to be given a shower and to get new clothes. Here men from the 632nd Quartermaster Battalion sort through wool shirts and trousers. The soldiers would turn in their old and dirty uniforms and receive an issue of different, but clean clothes. This led to some problems with sizes and keeping the correct insignia on, but was an efficient system designed to keep this assembly line cleaning moving at the fastest possible speed.

A French sailor points out the Eiffel Tower to two GIs from the 'Blue Star Commandos' (The Army Service Forces). The sergeant wears the first pattern fabric covered helmet liner with the horizontal white bar indicating he is an NCO. The private at right wears the standard helmet liner made from plastic.

WELCOME TO PARIS!

AMERICAN
RED CROSS
✚ CLUBS ✚

N°		CLUB NAME	STREET NUMBER	Tel. Number	Metro Station
✚ 0	D6	Central Registration Bureau	11, rue Scribe		
✚ 1	E8	Rainbow Corner	8, Boul. de la Madeleine	OPE 93-09	Opéra
✚ 2	E8	Columbia Club	2, rue de l'Élysée	ANJ 03-80	Madeleine
✚ 3	D8	Grand Central Club	10, Place de la Concorde	EUR 52-91	Concorde
✚ 4	E9	Independance Club (Or.)	39, Avenue de l'Opéra	ANJ 36-80	Saint-Lazare
✚ 5	E8	Lafayette Club (Officers)		ANJ 24-10	Concorde
				OPE 58-16	Opéra

N°	Key	CLUB NAME	STREET NUMBER	N
✚ 6	19	Left Bank Club (Negro-Staffed)		
✚ 7	E5	Mayflower Club (Off.)		
✚ 8	F8	Officers Club (Off.)		
✚ 9	D10	Pavilion Club for W.	1 bis, rue de Vaugirard	
✚ 10				

121

Left.
For most GI's the Eiffel Tower was the first sign they had reached the mythical city of Paris. Military Police such as these (with the white band around their helmet) were necessary in Paris as every American soldier wanted to visit this city. At one point it was estimated that there was the equivalent of a division's worth of men visiting Paris without permission. Most of these men just took a few days off from the war to see the sights and then returned to their unit, but this was a terrible drain on manpower.

Previous page
The Café George V on the Champs Elysées seems to be the place to drink a beer for these men from the 9th Air Force. The two men at right wear the British Made ETO jacket (first pattern). This was the precursor to the famous Ike jacket, and was mainly issued to Air Force troops in the ETO. The man third from the right wears the 2nd pattern ETO jacket with patch pockets on the chest. For comfort they have rolled their trousers up over the canvas leggings. The Technical Corporal on the left wears the sleeveless wool sweater (frequently made by Red Cross volunteers), the overseas cap, and carries a .45 pistol on his belt.

Right.
An anti-aircraft emplacement in front of the Palais de Chaillot, facing the Eiffel Tower. The crew of this 40mm gun has built a very nice emplacement out of stone blocks from the surrounding structures.

Right.
Two NCOs, a technical sergeant in an M43 field jacket on left, and a technician 4th class in an M41 jacket on the right, enjoy a glass of champagne on a boat on the river Seine. A technical sergeant (with three stripes up and two down) was the rank for most platoon sergeants. His M43 jacket is so new, the shiny water resistant cotton looks almost like leather.

Below.
Ice cream was considered one of the things that GIs missed most, so it makes sense that they would be more interested in this stand than in the Notre-Dame Cathedral behind it. Both men wear the typical M41 field jacket and wool trousers. At the far right is a medic (with the Red Cross arm band pinned to his sleeve) who wears a paratrooper jacket.

Below.
A few GIs on leave in Paris pose for a photo taken in front of the Arc de triomphe du carrousel, in the Tuileries gardens of Paris. They are quite typically dressed in M41 jacket, wool trousers, leggings and helmet liner.

Right.

This M16 half-track with quad mounted .50 caliber machine guns guards the Place de la Condorde in Paris. The vehicle crew wears the winter combat jacket with knitted collar and cuffs. This jacket was much warmer than the standard field jacket when riding in an open vehicle. Visible in this photo are three metal beam obstacles known as 'Belgian gates'. These were anti-tank obstacles made by the Germans. They are best known for their use as anti-invasion obstacles on the Normandy beaches, but as shown here were used inland as a portable roadblock.

Below.

This lucky GI from the First Army is taking an enlisted WAC for a ride in a bicycle-powered cab. He wears the M41 jacket, wool trousers, and the helmet liner. She has on the winter OD wool WAC uniform. Her hat looks more like a small sized man's garrison cap than the WAC garrison cap. WACs in the ETO were constantly short of uniform items and had to make do with many small sized men's uniforms.

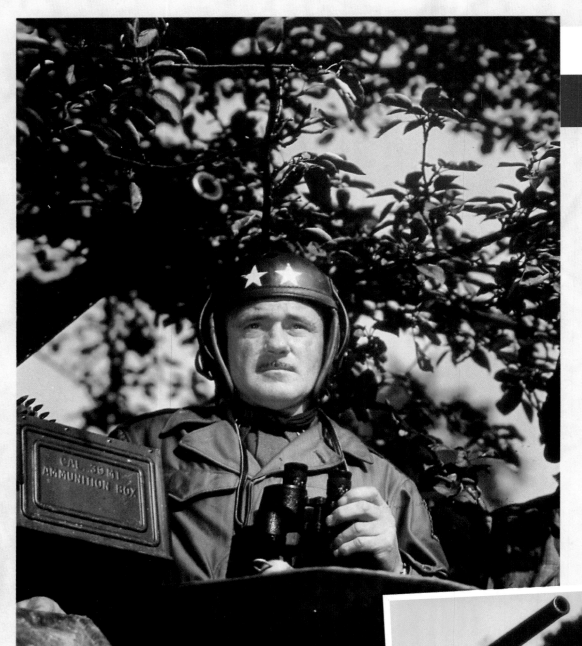

Opposite.
Four Star General George Patton was photographed while in command of the 3rd Army (note insignia on helmet and left shoulder). He wears four horizontal overseas stripes on his sleeve denoting 2 years of overseas service in WW2, and four chevrons below indicating two years overseas service in WW1 (each stripe stands for six months). He wears the following ribbons: Bronze Star, Distinguished Service Cross, Distinguished Service Medal, Silver Star, Purple Heart, and a foreign decoration presented to him by the Sultan of Morocco. The Bronze Star is out of the correct order of precedence, and has probably just been awarded. Patton wears the 'Ike' Jacket, which due to the small number of these jackets that arrived in Europe before the end of the war, was considered an officer's uniform. When it was later issued to all enlisted men, officers preferred to have a dark chocolate brown version to set them apart.

Above and right.
Major General Ernest Harmon was the Commander of the 2nd Armored Division during the Battle of the Bulge. These two photos were taken before his promotion to Lieutenant General and commander of the XXII Corps in January 1945. In one he rides his command tank with the two stars of a Major General painted on his tanker's helmet. He wears the M43 field jacket - the winter combat jacket was more commonly seen on tank crews. A 2nd Armored Division patch can be barely seen on his left shoulder. In the other photo he stands next to his command tank, as indicated by the red plate with two stars. He wears stars on his shirt collar, on his helmet, and on the jacket shoulder straps.

GIs and GENERALS

Right.
Lieutenant General Courtney Hicks Hodges was the commander of the First Army in France. This photo shows him in his Ike jacket with the dark green 'combat commander' stripes worn under the stars on his shoulder straps. These stripes were worn only by officers who had a direct combat command (not by supply or administrative officers). His ribbons are for: the Distinguished Service Cross, Distinguished Service Medal with oak leaf cluster (two awards), Silver Star, Bronze Star, Mexican Service, WW1 Victory with three stars, Purple Heart, American Defense, ETO with three stars, and then three foreign decorations that include the Croix de Guerre with Palm.

Below.
Major General Clarence Huebner, commander of the First Infantry Division, stands amidst dragon's teeth of the Siegfried Line. This heroic pose shows him wearing the winter combat jacket with a .45 pistol in the standard shoulder holster. He has the 1st Division insignia painted on his helmet, as did most men from his division. He commanded the 'Big Red One' from July 1943, until his promotion to V Corps commander in January 1945.

Below.
More junior officers became casualties in the ETO than the US Army could replace through standard officers' training programs. Many outstanding soldiers were given battlefield commissions to 2nd lieutenant to make up for the shortage in officers. In the Fall of 1944 a school was set up at Fontainebleau, France to provide a crash course in becoming an officer. Men selected for superior performance on the battlefield were sent here to train to become a combat officer, then commissioned and sent into combat. As these men had already proven themselves on the battlefield, they tended to be very good combat leaders. This photo shows the bazooka firing range at Fontainebleau with officer cadets shooting the two-piece M9 bazooka.

Above.

Men from the 1108th Engineer Battalion try a new approach to clear a mine field. The have tied yellow primacord (which is filled with explosives) to the tail of an M6A3 bazooka round. The black tube that the bazooka round comes in has been split down to make a firing ramp. The bazooka round will be fired with a battery, and hopefully, will carry the primacord over the mine field. Then the engineers will detonate the primacord in hopes that all land mines within a few feet will be set off by the explosion. The major drawback to this method was that some mines would be far enough away form the blast to not detonate, but close enough to be damaged by the shock. This left them particularly dangerous to disarm, as they could explode at the slightest touch.

Above.
A WC-51 3/4 ton Dodge truck bearing a red cross stops in a path cleared through some dragon's teeth. This size truck, both with and without a winch, was commonly referred to as a 'weapon's carrier'. The truck shown here bears no unit markings on its bumper, which is unusual. It does carry the names of the driver and co-driver just under the windshield. In the background can be seen the WC-54 closed cab ambulance. This was based on the same chassis as the WC-51, but had an enclosed cab and hard body on the rear. The rubble strewn around the road is from the demolition of the concrete obstacles, which was normally accomplished with a bulldozer or tank dozer.

Left.
Soldiers were not permitted to fraternize with German civilians, but the rules did not extend to German dogs. This GI from the 37th Infantry Regiment, 9th Infantry Division seems to have found a friend just across the German border. He wears double buckle combat boots, and a wool shirt over the high necked sweater. His trousers could be either HBT fatigues or the cotton M43 field pants. The fine webbed net on his helmet is one of many different patterns that were used by American soldiers. The children are surprisingly well kept and clean.

Labelled as being 'on the Siegfried Line', this shot shows a typical soldier crouching under the roots of a fallen tree. He is using the EE-8 field telephone, and the large DR-4 wire reel is visible in the lower left corner. His scarf is made from the camouflaged silk of a parachute. This was a trendy thing to do when the material could be obtained. Like most combat GIs he needs a shave, but his uniform is much too clean for anyone that has spent any time on the front lines. His trousers still hold a crease, and there is only a small amount of dirt on the knee. This was probably a well-posed shot for the folks back home, using a GI that looked just dirty enough to be real.

Above.
The US Army was poorly equipped to fight in the cold and snow of the Ardennes. This was mainly due to a lack of port facilities, which meant that most of the cold weather clothing was still on ships waiting to be unloaded. It was not until January 1945 that most combat units in Europe started to get their winter uniforms. This patrol, from the 7th Armored Division, moved through St Vith for this staged photograph. The men are too bunched together to be anywhere near the enemy. Very close inspection of the shot shows what looks like the telltale breast pockets of the British snow suit. Some US units were issued with British white camouflage in the ETO, while many snow suits were made locally from whatever white cloth was on hand.

Left.
Troops of the 7th Army coming up from Italy were much better equipped for cold weather. Their quartermasters had lots of experience with cold weather, and made sure that they had plenty of warm uniforms on hand well before the winter set in. This soldier models the latest in winter uniforms: the parka which reversed from white to a light shade of OD, the pile cap with warm earflaps, the trigger finger mitten outer shells (worn over a wool liner), M43 pants, and shoe-pacs. Unfortunately, his counterpart in the Ardennes did not have access to these items until after the main fighting had ended.

The 551st Parachute Infantry Regiment was photographed in a series of shots taken in the snow of the French Alps and this is proof that skis were used in the ETO. The Army had two units that were specially trained for combat in the snow: the 10th Mountain Division, and the First Special Service Force. These units were never really used for specialized mountain operations.

Left.
Here an 81mm mortar from the 551st is shown firing white phosphorous shells. White tape has been wrapped around the mortar tube to camouflage it. The gray chemical shells use the black plastic fuses. The crew wears the reversible ski parka with fur trim on the cuffs and hood. The fur acted as a barrier keeping warm air inside the parka, but this version was expensive to produce, so most late war parkas were made without the fur.

Bottom left.
A close up of a sniper from the 551st in the French Alps. He is armed with the 1903 A4 Springfield rifle. This sniper version of the Springfield had a telescopic sight, with the standard iron front sights removed. One man from every infantry platoon was supposed to be armed with this sniper rifle. The constant turnover in riflemen meant that this was not always the case. The 1903 A4 was much more accurate than an M1 Garand, but men trained on the semi-automatic Garand tended to prefer it over the bolt action Springfield.

Above.
One of the bridges set up in the Remagen area was this one built by the 552nd Heavy Pontoon Battalion. Assigned to the IIIrd Corps, the bridge is shown here guarded by MPs with the IIIrd Corps insignia on their helmets. The MPs wear the M43 jacket, combat boots, and both have a plastic OD whistle fastened to their chest pocket. The yellow sign saying 'class 24' refers to the weight class of the bridge. Part of the MP's job was to check every vehicle to make sure the bridge classification number on every vehicle did not go over 24. This number was always painted on a round yellow marker fixed to the front passenger side of every vehicle.

Below.
Further to the south vehicles of the 7th Army cross this pontoon treadway bridge at Worms Germany. It has been named after their commander: General Alexander Patch. No unit markings can be seen on any of the vehicles, but the bridge was clearly built by the 85th Heavy Pontoon Battalion. Two men at the bottom right look like they might have 75th Division insignia painted on their helmets. The photo was captioned as being taken on 28 March 1945, which falls into the same time period that the 75th Division was crossing the Rhine.

As the Germans retreated they left behind them a wake of destroyed ports and bridges. The divers of the Port Construction Companies were mainly used to clear harbors of sunken ships and booby traps. They were forced to remove booby traps that were set in water that offered little or no visibility. This diver from the 1058th Port Construction Company is preparing to check out the footings of a railroad bridge in Aachen. He has no way of knowing if German engineers have booby trapped the underwater supports. His assistant wears a captured German pistol. This was popular for troops behind the lines, but not commonly seen in combat.

Inset.
Troops from the 314th Infantry Regiment (79th Infantry Division) prepare to cross the Rhine at Orsoy Germany in assault boats and LCVPs. The LCVPs were brought up to the front lines on Army tank transporters. This was one of the only times in the war that Navy LCVPs were painted olive drab. On the left one soldier is seen wearing his M41 field jacket, and carrying a dark colored, OD#7 shade, lightweight gas mask bag. The small boats in the foreground are Army Engineer assault boats. Sitting in one of them is a soldier with the standard Army inflatable life belt.

Supporting the crossing of the Rhine in boats was this smoke generating company making a smoke screen. A mixture of oil and chemicals, called 'fog oil', was sprayed onto a hot surface resulting in a thick white cloud. Some smoke screens were used to fool the Germans into thinking the Americans were crossing the Rhine, when in fact they were making the crossing at another location. Most smoke screens were used to hide ground troops from aerial attacks or observation.

Above.
As the war in Europe came to an end, Germans surrendered in such large numbers that the Allies had a hard time taking care of them. This photograph shows German vehicles and troops taken prisoner on the Czechoslovakia Border in May 1945. This excellent shot shows a wide variety of German vehicles in their late war camouflage colors.

Above.
In Berchtesgaden, 'Smiling Al' Kesselring of the German Air Force shares a laugh with General Anthony McAuliffe, Commander of the 101st Airborne Division. It is hard to imagine that just days before these men were trying to kill each other. McAuliffe is wearing the Ike jacket with dark shade pants and paratrooper boots. The 101st was sent south to secure Berchtesgaden in case some German troops decided to try and hold out after the surrender.

Right.
Major General Clarence Huebner, former commander of the 1st Infantry Division, was promoted to commander of the Vth Corps by the end of the war. The 69th Infantry Division was under his Corps command when they made the first contact with Russian troops on the Elbe River. He is seen here with a souvenir Soviet Army flag presented to him by his opposite number. A comparison of ribbons worn in the previous photo of him (see page 128), and this post war photo, reveals a number of new foreign decorations. At the end of the war there was a frenzy of awarding medals to senior Allied commanders. Huebner wears a Soviet Guards badge for which he was probably made an honorary member.

Right.
Belonging to the 81st Cavalry Reconnaissance Squadron - 1st Armored Division, this M24 Light Tank rolls through a village in ruins on the road to Bologna, in April 1945. A Thompson SMG hangs on the turret side, its stock has been removed for ease of handling inside the tank.

Bottom.
After the war many GIs were given a chance to visit Switzerland, which had remained untouched by the war. This GI seems to be much more interested in the Swiss woman than in the offered postcard. He wears the Ike jacket with an open wool shirt. This was against regulations, and he should have been wearing a tie. The red piping on his garrison cap indicates he is an artilleryman.

Bottom right.
These happy men are toasting the fact that this is their last coffee and doughnuts in the ETO. The unit is ready to board a ship to return back to the States. Men were selected to return by way of a points system. Points were assigned for time in service, having children, and number of wounds and decorations. Men with high point totals went home first. This meant that combat units were broken up to group men with similar point totals together for the voyage. Some soldiers were transferred dozens of times before finally ending up in the group they would go home with.

141

Above.
The 1st Infantry Division was given the job of providing guards for the Nuremburg trials. These men from the 18th Infantry Regiment have spared no effort to look as sharp as possible. The officer with his back to the camera wears a Nuremburg District Patch, which is also seen on the white helmet liners. Not only were belts and holsters white, but just behind the first guard can be seen a white night stick. In the front row of prisoners is Herman Göring wearing his trademark dove gray uniform.

Left.
As the fighting came to an end the Allies realized that there was going to be a great shortage of adequate shelter for POWs, displaced civilians, and American soldiers. Prefabricated wooden huts were ordered from Switzerland, and once Germany surrendered, the huts were shipped to different camp locations. German POWs, such as seen here, were used to assemble these buildings. Most of the POWs were glad just to be fed and housed- not to mention just having lived through the war. They continued to wear their German uniforms, but generally removed all military insignia.

Above.
Men of the 334th Artillery Battalion, 87th Infantry Division, are seen here at Camp Oklahoma City preparing their 105mm howitzers for the long voyage back to America. This is just one of many tent cities set up to hold returning servicemen. Their helmets are all painted with the golden acorn insignia of the 87th Division. Once the war ended, more and more units began to paint their insignia on helmets.

GOING

Left.
The last sight before the leaving the Theater is a final check by MPs. One MP is resplendent in his white helmet, leggings, and British Made belt and shoulder strap. His partner doesn't quite look the part and was given this assignment as temporary duty until he too received orders for home. The 84th 'Railsplitter' Division patch is worn on the right shoulder. When men were transferred out of units they had fought in combat with, they hated to remove their beloved patch. The Army finally approved of wearing 'battle patches' of units on the right shoulder, upon transfer to a different unit. The insignia of the unit currently assigned was always supposed to be worn on the left shoulder, but in the confusion of the first few months after the war this was not always followed. No one wanted to tell a combat veteran he had to take off the insignia of a division he had fought with.

Above.
Some strange insignia was seen on men returning from the ETO. This man with an 8th Air Force patch wears paratrooper wings with a bronze star. The star signifies a combat jump. The blue piping on his garrison cap means he is an infantryman, but the collar disk shows Army Air Corps. Possibly he made one combat jump, was wounded, and ended up in the 8th Air Force at a desk job. The blue 'G' button is a temporary marker showing his status for the ship returning home.

HOME

Above right.
Another photo from the series of men going home shows a sergeant with an Airborne Troop Carrier patch. He has spent 2 years overseas as indicated by his four 'hash marks' (service stripes). The Number '3' button shows his ship status. The object behind his head is part of a life preserver.

Right.
These two members of the Army Air Force seem quite happy to be going home. The WAC wears what is probably a small sized man's Ike jacket. She wears the ribbons for the Good Conduct, WAC, and ETO medals. Her companion wears the first model British made ETO jacket and an aviation mechanic's cap.

Corporal Charles Hannon was one of many men that left the ETO with a heavy heart. He knew he would have only a stopover in America on his way to the Pacific. He was one of the two million men being shipped from Europe to a bloody invasion of Japan. Casualties for the invasion of Japan were predicted to run over a million men. The dropping of the A-bomb and the surrender of Japan made a lot of American soldiers very happy. Cpl. Hannon carries his duffle bag, carbine, and lightweight gas mask bag. Around his neck can be seen the M–1944 combat pack straps.